You've Got a Story

and it's better than you think!

Stephen Bransford

You've Got a Story and it's better than you think!
Copyright ©2020 by Stephen E Bransford

ISBN: 979-8-63348-942-2

All rights reserved. No part of this publication may be reproduced or transmitted in any form or by any means without written permission from the publisher.

All scripture verses are taken from the New King James Version of the Bible (NKJV). New King James Version®. Copyright © 1982 by Thomas Nelson. Used by permission. All rights reserved.

Editor: Renée Gray-Wilburn

Cover design/Interior design: Satoshi Yamamoto

Printed in the United States of America.

To my wife, Meganne.
Her private story towers over anything I have written.

Table of Contents

Foreword 7

Preface 9

Chapter One Your Private Story 11

Chapter Two Your Public Story 23

Chapter Three What Makes a Good Story Good? 49

Chapter Four What Makes a Good Story Bad? 69

Chapter Five Publishing Strategy 79

Chapter Six A Final Word 103

About the Author 109

Foreword

When the Lord added Stephen Bransford to my staff in 1999, it was one of the greatest gifts He's ever given me. Not only has he directed my Media Department for the last 21 years, but his fingerprints are all over my ministry. He is a gifted communicator.

Although he has helped me and other large ministries in the area of telecommunications, his real passion is storytelling. As you will learn in this book, he is not only an award-winning novelist, he has also ghost written autobiographies, which have sold tens of thousands of copies.

If you have a desire to get your story on paper and get it published, you need this book. It will not only aid you in writing it, but the information on publishing and distribution is invaluable. Stephen's lifetime love of writing has given him a unique ability to analyze and understand what makes a story work. In this book, you will gain insight into the fundamentals that will help you bring your story to life.

Finally, this book brings home the idea that, beyond the writing process, your story is a dynamic spiritual journey that never ends. As Stephen says, "YOU'VE GOT A STORY, and it's better than you think."

Andrew Wommack
Founder & President, Andrew Wommack Ministries

Preface

My advice in this book is addressed to writers who believe in God. Furthermore, this book is targeted to those, like me, who believe in the Ultimate Story. We see God as a loving heavenly Father, who plans to restore His wayward children, and Jesus Christ as His Son, given as the only acceptable sacrifice for the sin of the world. All human stories are absorbed into this one—the vile, the sublime, and everything in between.

Beyond mere belief (even devils believe and tremble), I relate my storytelling techniques to people who know that God actively talks to them by His Spirit, though not necessarily in an audible voice. They also know that they can talk back to Him in real relationship, not just in formal religious prayer.

If you are uncomfortable with these ideas, this book is not for you. The ideas that set me free may strike you as ignorant or repugnant. The things I consider precious, you may find distasteful. Why should either of us waste our time in a book about the cosmic importance of your story? I'm saying that our stories have real significance *only* in relationship to God.

On the other hand, let's say you have responded in faith to receive Jesus as your Savior. Maybe it was long ago, or perhaps it was recently. Maybe you read the Bible and had a transforming response to God's love. In this case, you are born again. God's Spirit is alive in you. We have something in common. You are a new creation in Christ, and this not only begins your endless relationship with God, but your story suddenly takes on a higher meaning. You were in Christ from the foundation of the world.

Now that's a story worth telling.

Chapter One

YOUR PRIVATE STORY

I could tell she had a lot on her mind. She twisted a Kleenex between her fingers and hung around as others told me how much they had enjoyed my talk. Draped in layers of clothing that disguised a post-middle-aged body, she had short-cropped, dishwater blonde hair with flecks of gold and gray, and a sad but pleasant face with no makeup. She waited until all the others were gone.

"I have a story," she said, "and I think I should write a book."

"OK," I said, always ready to encourage a new writer. "Describe your story in a nutshell."

"I was married for thirty years to a man I never knew."

"Sounds painful, sad."

"It was a bad marriage. No communication, no real affection, no children. Not long ago, he told me he wanted to leave to be with his lover."

I visualized her husband chasing a trophy wife. "So, what was it like to finally learn the truth?"

You've Got a Story

"The truth is," she said, twisting the Kleenex as if strangling something, "his lover was another man."

So much for my trophy wife speculation. I searched for something to say. "Maybe that's a book," I said. "I think a lot of people would be interested to know how you dealt with it."

"It's happening to more people these days. I'm not alone. But I don't think I really *dealt* with it. We separated but never divorced. A few months ago, his lover called to tell me he had died of a heart attack."

"Dear Lord! You must be hurting."

"Not really."

I was beginning to see that if nothing else, this story was still in process. "So, were you able to learn anything? Were you able to talk to him before he died?"

"No. It was sudden."

"Did you have any takeaways?"

"Well, I learned how to do the good Christian thing. At the funeral, his lover sat next to me sobbing through the entire service. I took his hand and patted it, trying to keep him calm. The weird part is, I had no tears myself. I have not felt one ounce of sadness for my husband."

I could imagine a bunch of reasons why. "So, you want to write this sad story in a book?"

"Yes."

"Why?"

She was now ripping her Kleenex apart. Finally, she spoke with an edge of anger, "Maybe it's for the other women who have gone through this."

"Yes. I'm sure you would have an audience with them. But I believe there's a much larger audience out there that could benefit from the lessons you will eventually see in this tragedy. So maybe it's not yet a book for the world to read. Think about it."

SELF-DISCOVERY

We all have a story. I believe every story, good and bad, needs to be recorded so that we can revisit it over the years. This is part of the process of realizing all that we were meant to be in Christ. Within the scope of each story there are thresholds, turning points, setbacks, defeats, successes, triumphs, mistakes, lessons, and mysteries. These are woven together by God's overarching purpose to reveal the tapestry of His work in our lives. These can be valuable lessons to share with the world. But any fresh tragedy, trauma, or other significant event needs to be examined and re-examined over time before we can see it clearly enough to bring out its treasures.

Unfortunately, most important story details are frittered away and forgotten by neglect. Few people pay attention. Few keep a journal of their lives. On the other hand, when terrible events overtake some people, they want to broadcast the gory details immediately. It is like their howl of anger and pain. Others want to forget it. (And for a time, forgetting it can be the best policy.) But with the Holy Spirit's guidance, sooner or later the good and bad of our past becomes relevant to the present, offering us the keys to a better future. That is when our story becomes publishable. But we only know this if we pay attention, and journaling is one of the best ways to pay attention.

I'm reminded of the first book God told someone to write in the Bible. The story is found in Exodus 17:14—"And the Lord said unto Moses, 'Write this for a memorial in a book ….'" God was aware of the need to remember, and He ordered a book written for that purpose.

Writing notes as we go can help us see ourselves more accurately in time. We can appreciate our story more perfectly after years have passed and we have forgotten many of the written details of our experience. Eventually, we see a grand design and pattern, and realize that the events of our lives are not accidental. They are full of growth, time-tested wisdom, and valuable lessons. And they can help us better appreciate our journey with Him.

PUBLIC EXPOSURE

Publishing our story for the world to read is another matter. When we decide to publish, it should be in response to God's call, not part of our personal therapy. We need to let plenty of time pass. Time doesn't heal. Perspective heals, but it takes time to gain perspective. When our story is fresh with raw emotion, we lack perspective, the kind of intelligent view that will really help others on their journey. We should ask God for guidance here: "What part of my story do You want me to share? Is this the right time and place to share it?"

I didn't want to discourage the woman with the Kleenex, but she had no idea the grueling task ahead of her, nor how very far she was from the finish line. I told her, "I think your story is very important. There is something in it that needs to be shared with the world, but I don't think you know what it is yet. It's not just about what happened to you, it's also about what you believed when it happened. It's about what you thought, what you felt, how you prayed or stopped praying, how you responded, and how you were changed. It's about the ups and downs and lessons you learned along the way. It's OK that you don't know these things yet. That's perfectly normal under the circumstances."

She seemed thoughtful and ready to reconsider.

"Here's what I recommend," I said. "Before this story can be something for the world, it needs to be something for you. Just you. You need to get this entire story out of your head and on paper. If you're a talker, get a digital recorder and talk it out. Hold nothing back. Let it fly—the good, the bad, and the ugly. Do not censor yourself. Then transcribe it. There's more in your story than you've ever dreamed, but it's all dammed up inside of you. Right now, you're unable to see the bigger picture. You're a wonderful person with a unique story, and it's better than you think. Take your time."

THE BIRTH OF A DREAM

I spoke from experience. From the age of sixteen, I had dreamed of writing a great American novel. The dream began in 1966 when my high school English teacher held up the celebrated novel, *Elmer Gantry*, by Sinclair Lewis. A few years earlier, the book had been made into an Academy Award-winning movie starring Burt Lancaster.

"This is an example of great American storytelling," my English teacher said. "It's a story about a preacher. A religious hypocrite."

I opened the book and read the first line: "Elmer Gantry was drunk."

That was enough for me. I slammed the book shut. Why would the entire literary establishment, not to mention Hollywood, celebrate a story about a two-faced preacher?

My father was an upstanding Assemblies of God preacher without a hypocritical bone in his body. I began dreaming of writing a novel about a preacher who was true to his calling. A novel that would turn the tables on the literary establishment. Perhaps one day a high school English teacher would hold my book up for a new generation of students as an example of truly great storytelling. Perhaps there would be a movie. Maybe even an Academy Award! Why not? And why not me?

Like the lady twisting the Kleenex, however, my dream was driven by immature thoughts and emotions. In high school, I was simply a half-baked preacher's kid with a hypersensitivity to hypocrisy (having never experienced my own). The literary celebration of Elmer Gantry made me angry. Writing my own novel was a worthy dream, but anger alone would never drive me to the finish line. Nevertheless, God used this brief moment of teenaged wrath to set me on the road to a marvelous destiny.

THE PATH OF A DREAM

Every dream must navigate a minefield of challenges. My first reality check, of many to come, occurred immediately. No high school English teacher worth his salt would grade me for the quality of my ambitions. I was graded strictly on performance. That teacher, so impressed with Sinclair Lewis, was less than impressed with me. I earned nothing but C's in his class. My first reality check showed that I was far from being a great American novelist.

Eighteen years later, however, I stood before a packed crowd in the Anatole Hotel in Dallas to receive the Texas Literary Festival Award for fiction. This prize was awarded for my novel, *Riders of the Long Road*. At last, I had achieved my dream with a fictional story about Silas Will, a circuit-riding preacher accused of scandal, who proved true to his calling. Doubleday New York had published it, and Evelyn Oppenheimer, a leading literary critic, had nominated it for the award.

My preacher-father had been flown to Dallas for the ceremony, and during my acceptance speech, I introduced him to the literary crowd. I told them he was the inspiration behind the character of Silas Will. He received a warm ovation.

Best of all, a few months later I returned to my hometown as an award-winning novelist. My visit was hosted by the main street bookstore. The first guest through the door was my high school English teacher, now retired. He was also the last to leave, asking for an autographed copy of *Riders of the Long Road*.

"Of all my students," he said, "none went on to have a novel published, let alone an award-winning novel. In a million years, I would never have guessed you would be the one." After a pause, his eyes grew moist. "What did I miss?"

"You didn't miss anything," I said. "I earned C's in your class. I was not a good writer in high school."

"But I should have seen something. I missed the chance to say that I knew talent when I saw it."

"Well, I'm not so very talented, sir. Getting published has been about the hardest work I've ever done. What you did is that you lit a fire in me back in high school. All these years later, that fire has never gone out. Thank you."

MILESTONE OF FAILURE

So, what changed during those eighteen years between high school and winning a literary award? In short, I discovered the power of my own story.

Today, I am approached by many people, like the woman twisting the Kleenex, who have a dream of writing their life story or a novel based on their life story. I tell them they are on the right track. "You must write about what you know, and your own story is the best place to start."

In my case, the dream of writing that great American novel got stuck for many years after high school. Memories of being told that I was an average writer kept me sidelined with fear. I didn't want to fail at the thing I loved so much. Finally, driven by self-loathing and ambition, I decided that I would force myself to write something significant *or die!* Rather than begin with the novel of my dreams, I turned inward to unload the pent-up story of my thirtysomething life so far. It was really all I had at the time.

Willing myself forward, I wrote a passionate tell-all of my coming of age in the home of a Pentecostal preacher. I titled the book, *Holy Roller*, in an attempt to attract curious, and perhaps hostile, readers. Many people despised the religious subculture that I knew so well. I felt driven to open their eyes to a bigger picture. I wanted them to see the complex mix of spiritual and human qualities that flourished in American Pentecostalism. Through my story, and through my eyes, I wanted to help them see beyond prejudice and ridicule.

The story included honest details about how I became emotionally screwed up through childhood blunders, made unbearable by an overload of religious guilt. It had resulted in a shattering mental and emotional breakdown in my early twenties. I chronicled the process of putting the broken pieces of myself together with the help of thorazine, psychotherapy, and the nonfiction sanity of C.S. Lewis. At the end of *Holy Roller*, I was able to show how my Christian convictions had not only survived—they had thrived! I felt that my story was worthy because I had not thrown the baby of faith out with the bathwater of ignorance. It was my hope that both a Christian and non-Christian reading audience would find my story eye opening, meaningful, and valuable.

I submitted the finished manuscript to Kays Gary, a trusted friend and a respected columnist for the *Charlotte Observer*. After reading it, he called me to his office.

He shook his head and finally spoke with great hesitation: "This...this is fascinating stuff, but I'm not sure... no, actually I have no idea who would publish something like this. I--- I think you needed to do this. I'm sure it was therapeutic, but don't put this out for publication. You'll regret it in a few years. You are young. Keep writing."

He had no idea—no, maybe he did—how he was crushing me with these words. I had invested all my spare time, energy, and money pushing my dream against the demands of being a husband, father, and provider. As I wrote, I had fantasized that this book would be critically acclaimed as a breakthrough and that I would be launched as a serious writer of serious material. If I hadn't dared to dream big as I wrote *Holy Roller* I would never have pushed hard enough to finish and reach this milestone. But now it seemed to be a milestone of failure.

PERSPECTIVE HEALS

Kays was right, of course. Time passed, and perspective grew. And today, that manuscript sits unpublished on a shelf in my home. I smile as I browse it from time to time, so glad I didn't publish it in all of its naïveté. What I know now is that the first mark you make in the publishing world often defines you for the rest of your career in the minds of your readers and peers. It will help you, or perhaps limit you, in everything that follows, and you should weigh the decision very carefully. That is what Kays Gary knew, and he was trying to help me avoid regret.

The passing of time has also revealed that my unpublished life story was better than I thought. It was better in ways I did not imagine as I wrote it. Among other things, it has shown me the immature roots of my own thinking, my behavior, my writing style, and my personality. It has visualized my invisible patterns of belief so that I see how some of my qualities have been strengths and others weaknesses that have affected my relationships and my career.

To this day, I continue to grow as a writer and as a human being. In the process, I look back at my manuscript and see those parts of me that have changed and those that needed to grow. I also see those things that did not change and should never change. I continue to be humbled by this process. It reminds me that God is not through with me yet. This is priceless foundational information that I would never possess without having written that very first raw story of my life. The unpublished document has found its place as a personal journal that lives and breathes between God and me.

THE SOURCE

As a professional communicator, today I appreciate how *Holy Roller* has remained my seminal statement, my unique wellspring of inspiration. The themes that I began to express in that story have provided the bloodstream of my creative expression down through the years. There is not a project I undertake that my life story does not inform in some essential way.

This is why I say that everyone has a story that should *not* be told. A story that should be written and left on the shelf. This is your story, the one that is just for you. It is your treasure. It is actually the story of Christ in you, and of your life in Christ. It is deep. So deep that it is quite beyond you. By attempting to write and understand it, you may never achieve your goal of being published, but more importantly, you will never stop growing toward God's purpose in your life. It will help you appreciate the stories of others, too. The story you never tell is in many ways the most important story of all.

Finally, your story is better than you think because ultimately, it is not your story. You are God's story, His testimony, His workmanship. He is painting a picture of Himself on the canvas of you, a reality that is as unique as your fingerprints, retina scan, and DNA. It includes all of your worst and best days and everything in between—much of which you have forgotten.

I hope you will learn to delight in your untold story, because, believe me, your heavenly Father does. He not only loves you, He's your Creator, and He has plans for you beyond your wildest dreams. And one day in heaven, you will be face to face with Him. You will know as you are known, and He will publish your story in all of its radiant fullness. Then your eyes will be opened to see that He has worked everything in your life for your good and for His greater glory.

You have a story, and it's better than you think.

Chapter Two

YOUR PUBLIC STORY

Once you have delivered your life story to words on the page, save it, make a backup copy, and leave it. Go away and forget it for as long as you like. Days, months, years. It will not go away. It will be preserved like a time capsule as you follow new roads, learn new lessons, and meet new people. It will remain sealed until the day the Spirit of God hovers over the dark waters of your manuscript to call forth the testimony He wants to make of you.

How do you know when God is calling you to write? How do you discern His testimony from merely the stuff you want to say? There is no religious formula here. There is no three-step, six-step, twelve-step process to hearing the unmistakable voice of God. It is different for everyone, and it is utterly dependent upon your relationship with Him.

All I can say is you must listen for His voice. On your bed, in your car, at work, at play, in conversation, while watching TV, during a movie. Even in your dreams. Twenty-four/seven, He is speaking to you about everything, showing you that He is there and is the true Author of your life's story. But, if you are like most of us, every morning you are filling your head with the news of the day, the schedule you must keep, the bills you must pay, the phone calls you need to make, plans for the future, challenges coming at you. It can be impossible to hear His still, small voice through all of that noise.

HEARING GOD

Some believers only take time to tune in to God at church, but that misses the point of a round-the-clock relationship. Often at church, all that is heard is someone else's idea of what God is saying. The truth is, God is speaking to you one-on-one as surely as He is speaking to any religious leader. To hear for yourself, you have to practice listening with spiritual ears. *He who has ears to hear, let him hear.* Jesus often said this to the crowds following Him. He was not speaking to religious leaders. It's a word for everyone.

What you hear with your physical ears is probably not the voice of the Spirit. God's Spirit is within you during every circumstance, good or bad. But because of the nature of your flesh, it takes practice to pay attention. You can begin by asking God to make you sensitive to His voice. Paul writes that the flesh is at war with the Spirit. This is a violent opposition, and it clashes in your brain constantly. Training your spiritual ears to hear requires effort, focus, and discipline. Unless you try, you will simply be carried along by the trivial pursuits of life.

For me, the practice of hearing God often requires getting alone and becoming quiet. As the obligations of being a husband, father, and boss have consumed my energies, a wonderful quiet time has emerged for me. I fall into exhausted sleep at the end of the day only to awaken hours later to a quiet house and to a mind that has become clear. This is my prime time with God. I usually pick up my Bible and say, "Speak, Lord. I need to hear You."

Then I open the Bible and read a passage, sometimes Old Testament, sometimes New. Amazingly, the written Word comes alive, and I begin to hear thoughts that are not my own. I became hooked on this approach after hearing Andrew Wommack teach on the topic of *Effortless Change*. He illuminated the passage of Scripture in the book of Hebrews that speaks of the Word of God being alive and powerful, sharper than a two-edged sword. The living Word is more than a reading exercise. It does stuff to you. Once I understood and agreed that the Word of God was more than letters arranged on a page—that it was *alive*—I began to not just read my Bible but let it read me.

The passage in Hebrews goes on to say that the living Word pierces to the dividing of soul and spirit and discerns both the thoughts and secret intentions of the heart. As I continue to read and let the Bible read me, I see myself in ways I never knew before. The events of my life are reinterpreted in light of God's presence and person. Sometimes I just remain quiet, listening. Many insights begin to flow, and I use them as a springboard for conversation with God. Often, I am filled with joy and exhilaration, and in one way or another, end up worshipping my heavenly Father. I feel His pleasure during these episodes. I sense that He treasures these times even more than I do. The blessed effect of it tends to keep me in constant conversation with the Lord all day long about everything as it is happening. The good and the bad.

This experience is far more than a means to an end. In other words, it's not a way to become a successful writer or to gain blessing from God. It's not about gaining a publishing contract or getting a good story idea. It is a way of life. It is eternal life itself. It was God's reason for creation. It is what He is after with us.

In the Garden of Eden, He made man for the purpose of walking with him. Since the fall of Adam and Eve, very few of their offspring want to do that. Before the Flood, it was recorded that just two men, among the millions on earth, walked with God. They were Enoch and Noah.

I believe walking with God is for everyone today, and it is a completely naked journey. He knows the thoughts and intentions of our heart. We should not pretend fig leaves are hiding us. We have something better. The Lamb of God was slain to provide our covering. We should not waste His sacrifice. Rather, we should revel in the restored relationship He purchased for us and walk boldly with Him through everything, the best and the worst of our lives. He said, "I am the way, the truth, and the life." It's about a person. Without relationship with Him, we are merely religious.

You've got to understand that I am no spiritual giant. I am not putting myself on a pedestal here. In fact, in my sessions with the Lord, I often see more clearly how faulty and sinful I am in my natural condition. But the scripture tells me there is no condemnation with the Lord, and I do not have to become a better person to have a conversation with Him. That is good news, and that is my point. God has made this relationship available to everyone, everywhere, at all times. I encourage you to take advantage of it for yourself.

SHARING YOUR TESTIMONY

Out of the experience of walking with God, it becomes natural to see your story with new eyes. Ask the Lord what portion of it He might have you share. When you sense some idea of His answer, step out in faith and share it. Before a story is written, it should be told. That is what I recommend. Find those opportunities to tell about God's evidence in your life.

As you speak, carefully observe how it affects the listeners. He will sometimes speak to you through their responses. Be careful here, because the enemy will also attack you through their responses. Some people will find value in your story, others will be constructively critical, and still others will tear you to pieces. The scripture says not to cast pearls before swine because they will turn and rend you. The Lord will use the responses of people to sharpen your story and will never attack you. You have to learn the difference.

In this activity, remember, you are not sharing all the details of your private story. Those are the pearls that belong between you and your heavenly Father. In other words, you are not naked before people in the way that you are naked before God. Only He is worthy of that. Leave your "tell-all" on the shelf, and share only the portion of your story that you feel God is calling out for His good purposes. That leaves the responses of people in His hands, and there is no need to take offense when they do not receive your story in the way that you intend it. That is simply an indication that you need to work more on your presentation.

OPPORTUNITY KNOCKS

A strong indicator of God's direction for your story is opportunity. If you have no opportunity to share with others, it is unlikely that God is moving you to tell your story on a larger scale. But if people ask you to share your story, this can be a marker that God is calling your story out to minister to others.

Recently, I shared a portion of my story with my television production staff. Their numbers have grown, and in the course of working, they can forget that we are not just doing a job but are engaged in ministry. I feel it is my role to demonstrate what ministry means. In this case, I used some of my story to illustrate a few points. Afterward, I received thanks from several members of the crew, but one mature team leader came to me later and said, "That should be written in a book." As I left work that day, he reminded me, "Don't forget to work on that book."

I respected his opinion and took special note of his repeated comment. I also knew that much of the stuff that had come out of me in that meeting had first come to me in my night hours with the Lord. I had not planned to say it. Those kinds of spontaneous moments are in the zone of soul and spirit where only God is capable of working. He alone knows which elements will perform the work of His kingdom, and He prompts them from my memory at unexpected times and places.

The scripture says that I am His workmanship, and I believe it. I trust Him to use me when the time it is right. So, after my team leader's comment, I wrote a note of the things I had said and filed it away. I began asking God to make His way clear to me about how to proceed toward making my story public. Rather than writing immediately, I kept it for future reference. I recommend that you build and keep similar files.

At the time I made this note, I was writing this book and know that God did not intend to distract me with a separate vision. God has a time and place for every purpose under heaven, and we need to be willing to wait for it.

SEIZING OPPORTUNITY

In 1981, my older brother, Gordon, died in a tragic hunting accident. He was the eldest child of seven siblings, just thirty-four years old, a Vietnam vet, husband, father of four, and a legendary outfitter and hunting guide in the Bitterroot Wilderness of Northern Idaho. I was thirty-two at the time. In the years that followed, I sorted through the intense grief and drama of his untimely death. For a long time, I was too close to the emotional forest to see the trees. But slowly that began to change. I began to see patterns of God's love and grace in helping our family deal with the loss, and I shared portions of the story with friends and family, receiving very positive feedback.

Seven years later, I found myself producing television programs for James Robison's ministry in Texas. At that time, James, who was a world-class hunter and fisherman, wanted to publish a magazine called *The Christian Outdoorsman*. As the idea for the magazine took shape, Jim Ferguson, the editor, came to dinner at my home. I shared the story of going on the last elk hunt with my brother, during which I had created a photo album of his life and had distributed it to the family at Christmas. I had done this not knowing that a year later we would bury him.

You've Got a Story

In the years to follow, the album had become a treasure for the extended family. I took the photo album from the shelf and let Jim browse it. Immediately, he commissioned me to write the story for the inaugural issue of *The Christian Outdoorsman*. He also selected fourteen of the 35mm slides taken on the hunt to illustrate the story. One he chose to be the magazine cover. This was opportunity.

TAKING INVENTORY

Now began the hard part: I had to write it. For many hours I sat at my Kaypro II word processor, looking at the blinking cursor, wondering how best to present the story. Where to begin? I started by drawing on memories of the last elk hunt with my brother. To help the audience appreciate the making of the photo album, I began to go deeper. I recalled memories of our years growing up as competitive brothers in the home of an outdoorsman preacher we called Griz.

This process is something I call taking inventory. To tell the story I had to analyze what I had to work with. What were the elements of the story? As a more reliable resource, I retrieved *Holy Roller*, the original manuscript of my life story, and browsed the sections about growing up with Gordon and Dad. It turns out I had written many details that I had forgotten in the years that followed. I realized that some of these would add richness to the background of the hunting story. Once again, writing my tell-all story had not been a wasted effort. It now served as important research.

Storytelling is a lonely craft. You must cook up a good story before you can tell it, or write it. You must spend time alone in thought; time enough to let your imagination unfurl visions and scenarios from the meaning and facts of the story. It is amazing how many forgotten details will begin to return to your mind as you do this. You will suddenly realize you are not alone in the process. In fact, you are more engaged than ever in a conversation with your Maker. This is what I felt as I began to inventory elements for that article in *The Christian Outdoorsman*. It was a powerful confirmation that the Lord had directed me to this opportunity.

THE AUDIENCE

Inside the story of your life, and mine, are many smaller stories. Some of them will build the main story you are telling, others are beside the point. You want to keep the first kind and eliminate the others.

As I began to sort my stories, wondering what to leave in and what to leave out, I thought of the audience. This is essential for all good storytellers. The writer should establish in his mind who the audience is. There can be many categories of listeners and readers: men, women, children, families, singles, believers, unbelievers, friendlies, hostiles, members, outsiders, natives, foreigners. Who are they? Once you have established a profile of who your audience will be, I recommend that you begin to hear the story with their ears. I often visualize a reader's face when I write, trying to get inside his skin. As I unfold a scene, I am doing my best to reach my readers in the most powerful way possible. I want to see them laugh, cry, and not be able to put the story down.

Thinking about your audience, you might also want to see them with their chosen media. For example, imagine them not only with a book or a magazine, but possibly wearing headsets with an audio version of the story, reading a Kindle or other electronic device, using an ipad, laptop, desktop, or cell phone. You are not only available in these ways, you are in competition with others in the media. How do you win someone's attention to your story?

More importantly, within the media choices are applications that greatly limit the way your story can be presented, such as email, text, websites, blogs, YouTube, Facebook, Instagram, Twitter, and hundreds of new social media apps. Each platform requires that you adapt your story for the technology and the built-in preferences of the users. This is very important. Learn the various limits of each media application, and tailor your message to its intended audience. Some applications may not offer anything to benefit you. Ignore them.

Your story will most likely be delivered best in book form. The other media, however, can be used to find and motivate potential readers and buyers. You can direct them to your website, to Amazon, to an event where you will be speaking, or to wherever your book can be found. Writers today must think carefully about how to promote themselves in the new media, remembering that each one operates with its own set of rules for success.

In the case of *The Christian Outdoorsman*, my task was simpler. The internet and social media were unheard of back then. I knew that my main audience would be family-oriented men and women who wanted to see their faith at work in the arena of hunting elk. The magazine article would limit the length of my story to the editor's preference. I also knew that in the orbit of James Robison, there were many non-Charismatic believers. Few of them would care or understand the Pentecostal details of my upbringing. I wanted to reach them with the core lessons I had learned through this story. This meant that what I left out would be as important as what I included, and the Pentecostal details of my growing up were simply left out. This decision was about the audience. I felt God wanted me to appeal to the broadest group of readers possible.

STORY ARC

Next, I focused on the relationship between my brother and me. We had been opposites and rivals for all of our growing-up years. As the firstborn, he had been number one in just about every way. He had despised me and brutally persecuted me as the weaker brother in our youth. As I grew, I became focused on getting even with him. In everything from trivial pursuits to career paths, I became bent on beating him, asserting myself as number one, and rubbing his nose in it. It's a very old story called vengeance.

Since Cain and Abel, sibling rivalry has been a universal condition. But if my story had ended where it began, it would not have been worth telling. What made it special and rare was the marvelous healing of our relationship after Gordon's Vietnam years. God spoke. I changed. He changed. Putting aside our differences, we became brothers in ways brothers were meant to be. This is called story arc.

Like a rainbow, a good story must begin in one place and end in another. The ending can be a better place or worse, but in all cases, not the *same* place. Things that don't change are dead. Life moves. It improves. Or it goes bad. And yes, tragedy is also a worthy form of storytelling. Many lessons can be seen in tragedy.

Examine your story for its story arc. Trace the arc in an outline form. List the important details that capture the beginning condition of your story. Then describe the climax, or the main turning point of the story. Perhaps there are many incidents that bring change to the beginning condition, but the best stories pivot with a major dramatic climax. Find it. Describe it. Then describe the difference that it makes. This is your story arc.

CHARACTER ARC

Character arc is not the same as story arc. The story arc is the change of conditions from beginning to end, while the character arc is the internal drama that gives depth and meaning to the changes. Readers crave to know the difference a change makes to the characters of a story. How does it affect their thoughts, feelings, beliefs, and decisions? The arc moves from one internal state of being to another. This is not just the facts but what the facts mean to you, the writer. Without a character arc your story will not entertain the reader. Guaranteed.

In the story of my brother and me, I could not describe his internal drama. To give the story its full depth of meaning, I had to tell it from my own point of view. Writing from the author's point of view is called writing in first person. Only I knew the way my beliefs, thoughts, feelings, and actions had changed. This meant that the story was full of me. This did not mean that the story was *only* about me. But it was my job to carry water for the audience. Without my inner drama they would flounder with their own guesses and assumptions about everything.

As I wrote, I used personal pronouns: *I, me, my, mine*. Writing in first person is the very best way to make your personal story powerful for the reader. They travel, discover, and learn as you travel, discover, and learn.

PRECIPITATING ACTIONS

Clouds are made of water vapor, but that moisture doesn't become rain until it condenses into droplets large enough to respond to the pull of gravity. We call this transformation precipitation. Likewise, a story arc is full of the potential for change, but unless something happens to build tension toward the main climax, we do not have a story. We call these tension-building incidents precipitating actions. They influence the outcome, but they are not the main climax.

As I took inventory of the precipitating actions of my story, I began to notice an emotional pattern: Every action that did not directly involve the conflict between my brother and me caused the story to bog down. That's because those actions fell beside the point and did not build more tension into the conflict. The point of the story was my brother's persecution of me, my desire for vengeance, and my attempts to achieve it. In storytelling, conflict is good. It creates more tension for the climax to resolve.

You may say, "In my Christian life, everybody just loved one another. There was no conflict, no tension, no climax."

My response is that you have not adequately examined your story, especially your inner story. The beliefs, thoughts, and feelings that collided in your heart to make you the person you are today are connected to drama, relationships, decisions, and consequences. Let the Lord light up your hidden story. There have been conflicts against the strongholds of your mind and heart, as well as against the minds and hearts of others in your life. This is conflict. These things have made a great difference in your life and theirs. I think you could benefit from a few midnight hours discussing your story with God. He searches hearts. You are *His* testimony, and it involves more conflict than you think.

THRESHOLDS

Collect the emotional markers in your story, all the way back to your earliest memories of childhood if necessary. Each of us has a collection of memories that are dramatic, or perhaps traumatic, because of the emotions they have produced. Or, perhaps because of the emotions that produced them. In my midnight sessions with God, emotional memories are often dredged up, illuminated, and given deeper meaning. These moments become markers of the thresholds that I must cross in order to know God better and to know myself better. I suggest that you gather the emotional markers in your memory bank, and make note of them.

The emotional landscape of your life is both positive and negative. You should understand that an explosion of wonderful emotion will distort your judgment just as much as trauma will darken it. List as many of these markers as you can recall: ecstasy, depression, exhilaration, shame, innocence, guilt, arrogance, humiliation, greed, generosity, romance, rejection, love, terror, confidence, dread, and so forth. Each of these experiences is universal. Each has occurred at some moment for all of us in this fallen world. These emotional markers are so immensely powerful, we can feel overwhelmed by them and inadequate to deal with them, and so we bury them like dead puppies in the backyard of our minds.

But they never really go away. Sooner or later, when we are ready for the revelation, God will resurrect one of these moments, and in His presence, relive it in all of its overwhelming power. By trusting Him, we can cross a threshold into a new landscape of living. Whether blinded by ecstasy or wounded by pain, we see like never before how God works all things for our good. Even the memories we dread so much that we might rather die than face them. Trust God.

DEEP STUFF

I want to emphasize that these are not *necessarily* the details we should share in our stories, but this is how a storyteller becomes good at his craft. If you've ever read a story that just seems trivial and shallow, it is never a problem with the story itself; it is always because the storyteller has never gone deep enough. When you and God have examined the emotional markers of your life, you will no longer write shallow stuff in ignorance. The words you use and the way you unfold a story, the word pictures and the inner landscape you describe, all say to the readers that that they are in the hands of a worthy storyteller.

I have also discovered that these emotional markers are the reasons we do things we don't understand. I call this "acting on autopilot." These are besetting sins, little foxes of mysterious origin that trip us up again and again, no matter how we vow to eliminate them. "Why did I do that again, Lord? Why did I say that?" In the quietness of the midnight hour when your mind is clear, the God who searches hearts will lead you to answers. Each answer will involve an emotional marker that has distorted your beliefs. It will become a threshold for you to cross in your relationship with God. When you cross that threshold, you become a writer with depth.

TURNING POINTS

A threshold is something you cross when moving from one room to another, but a turning point is the place at which you change directions. Take inventory of the turning points in your story. These are mind changes, thought changes, belief changes. When these things change, your emotions and actions will always follow. This is as true as the smell of frying bacon. Turning points guarantee that your story is alive and well. If you describe them, and describe the difference they made in your life, your audience will be on the edge of their seats, learning lessons without knowing they are in school.

In writing the article for *The Christian Outdoorsman*, I described a key turning point at the very beginning. As I packed my gear for the upcoming elk hunt with Gordon, I described hearing the unmistakable voice of God. His specific instruction to me was, *Give your brother his place. Instead of competing with him on this elk hunt, celebrate his life.* I then described the impossible struggle that raged in my heart as my memories, beliefs, and emotions collided with this command from the Lord. In the end I was defeated. I confessed that I could not trust myself to obey His voice. I wanted revenge too much. That's when the story went deeper. God showed me the perfect vehicle that would discipline my natural responses to fulfill His purpose. This became the key turning point in my journey with God and my older brother.

VEHICLES

A story vehicle is an object or thought or thing that helps you obey God. His instructions to you may seem impossible. Your response is key. If you say, "OK, Lord, You can count on me," you are in trouble. Usually He asks you to do something that is quite beyond your natural abilities. It is important to be as honest as your deceitful little heart can be under the circumstances. I recommend that you surrender quickly and admit defeat. God does not end the conversation at that point. He will provide a way of escape—a crutch, if you will, to help you obey Him. This crutch is what I call a vehicle. Ask yourself if there is a vehicle in your story. If so, you have something powerful that you can share with the world.

    I remember in my youthful intellectual days hearing someone say, "Religion is just a crutch for weak-minded people." At first, I thought this sounded true. But in time, I came to embrace the idea of a crutch from God not as a liability but an asset. God's kindness is seen in the many crutches He mercifully supplies to those who know they can do all things *through Christ* and not through their own intellect or ability. When I described this vehicle at the first turning point of my story, the entire drama turned toward a much stronger conclusion.

In my story, the vehicle was a Nikon camera. I described in detail how God showed me how this camera would become the key to fulfilling His instructions. If I used the camera, instead of competing with my brother by using my big-game hunting rifle, I would be able to capture his unique life in pictures during this hunt. At the same time, I would give him his place and celebrate his life in a Christmas album of pictures that I would send to the extended family afterward. When I saw this clearly, I was able to build the drama around this vehicle that led to the unexpected climax of the story.

PATTERNS

Once you have assembled an inventory of story elements you may feel a bit lost. It will look like an impossible pile of details, and you may not know where to begin, how to proceed, or where to end. This is a good state of being. Again, it means that you can seek God to illuminate His will for your story.

Many times I have looked at an inventory that seemed bulky and disorganized, asking God for the story He would have me tell. As I have done this, something wonderful has happened. I've seen a pattern. It is a repeated lesson or problem or sequence in the pile of details that can be given a name. Perhaps the pattern is about guilt, forgiveness, social blunders, reconciliation, justice, mercy, hearing God, obedience, faithfulness, discipline, failure, worry, peace, ignorance, or self-discovery. The pattern was there all along, undiscovered.

Perhaps there are several patterns in the material, but until you have gathered the pieces together, the pattern remains invisible. Out of your inventory of story elements, collect the patterns and name them. Each theme will run like a thread from beginning to end in your story. This kind of multi-layered writing will turn a rather ordinary tale into a work of art. I see the patterns of writing like the patterns of life itself—beyond coincidence, they are the fingerprints of a caring God, performing the ultimate work of the Master artist.

CREATING AN OUTLINE

A good storyteller organizes his material before he begins writing. He takes the inventory of story elements and arranges them into an outline. This helps him see his material from beginning to end. The patterns of meaning can be noted along the timeline. This outline can be brief or detailed. I have created both types and worked with them, but I have never written for publication without one. Nor do I recommend it.

I would caution, however, that too much outlining betrays a problem. Some people are wired to create and follow an outline to the letter. This tends to result in a finished story that reads like a lecture. It may be accurate, but it feels academic and uninspired.

My outlines tend to be brief because I have learned that the real magic happens during the writing process. I have never delivered an outline exactly as I first wrote it. This is exciting to me. I have learned that I am not completely in charge of the story, so I don't pretend that my outline has to be perfect before I begin. A good story takes on a life of its own and overwhelms the structure. At this point the outline can change, and should change, to fit the inspiration. If the outline is obeyed to the letter, then true creativity will never show up.

THE DEFINING SCENE

Somewhere on your inventory list there is a defining scene or sequence. Look for it. This is a single incident that captures your character arc in a nutshell. It contains the internal state of your character at the beginning, and it demonstrates how your character is changed by the end. Is there something on your list that captures that journey in microcosm? This scene or incident is very likely to alter your neatly designed outline.

After days of writing, it suddenly came to me that the defining story in *The Christian Outdoorsman* article involved the incident of taking a particular picture of my brother. We had been riding in a pack train through the Idaho wilderness, and I had leaped from the saddle and run like a crazy man to get the shot. All the other hunters had made fun of me as I huffed and puffed in the high altitude to get into position ahead of the horses and riders. But months later, when the album came out, they all understood what I had done. Out of the hundreds of pictures that I had snapped on the elk hunt, this one captured my brother like no other.

In the magazine article, I reached inside myself to reveal the thoughts and feelings that had driven me to get this particular shot as I ran along the horse trail. I explained to the reader that I was responding to the voice of God instructing me to give my brother his place. Then I got into position and turned with my camera. I described the picture this way:

> He rode into view, filling the eyepiece from Stetson to chaps, a bearded, longhaired, outlaw of a man. Eyes narrowed, he fixed me from beneath his weathered hat brim. His right hand lightly held a braided horsehair rein while his left remained open in the loop of the lead line. Behind him the barren ridge stretched out, pierced along its way by steeplespired Engelmann spruce. He looked the part he played in life: a philosophical poetcowboy and Vietnam vet, who loved to sit under the stars with a shot of Jack Daniel's in his coffee, listening to coyotes howl, talking of Indian legend, archaeology, the origin of the species; and on rare occasions among family and friends, expounding his troubled understanding of God.

A year after taking it, this photo became celebrated as the last photograph of Gordon. As I recalled the effort and the sequence of taking the shot in detail, I knew this scene was the defining scene that would symbolize the reconciliation between my brother and me. I decided to begin the magazine story with that action sequence then flashback to flesh out the days that followed. It was an inspired idea that I believe came from God. The story went to another level.

WAR DANCE

All of the processes of research, inventory, and outlining are part of something I call "war dance." In primitive tribes, before going to war, the warriors would engage in a fierce dance around a bonfire, demonstrating their skills in martial arts. This was an important way of building courage to put their lives on the line in the actual battle to come. In my experience, there is a great temptation for writers to do the war dance forever—and never go to war.

    I joined a writers group in the 90s and was amazed to learn how many writers were hooked on college courses, writing seminars, instructional books, and endless inventorying, but never finishing a book. One fellow writer admitted to me, "I'm pathological. I'm terrified to finish a book and risk rejection." I sympathized but assured him a day of reckoning would come in which he would have to commit and put his finished manuscript on the market for better or worse. He eventually did it and became a successful author. The risk is real, but the reward of pushing past it can be amazing.

    I have to admit that I have loved the work of researching, inventorying, and outlining. But I must also admit that part of the reason I have loved it so much is that I can hide in the process. Over the years, I have been sorely tempted to let it go on forever. Why? Because it is a process filled with potential, and often with fantasies of bestselling success. Sooner or later, however, it becomes time to face reality. Life demands that I write and put myself on the line. Perhaps none of us is as good as our fantasies. Even so, we must take the risk of finding out. I believe that we must be willing to fail at the thing we love most in order to become a truly good storyteller.

Brace yourself. There are no shortcuts. The risk is real. This can be a gut-wrenching ordeal, and the outcomes will not always be victorious.

GOING TO WAR

Your first outline may not make the final cut. This is normal. Give it some downtime. Sleep on it. Rewrite it. Do it all over again, and do it all over again *again*. Tweak it. Finally, when you see a vision for how the whole story might work, step out in faith and begin to write.

Write this vision of the story from your heart. Do not hold back. Unleash the full story that has come to your mind. This is the first rough draft, and there will be plenty of time for you to critique it later. But if you don't finish a draft, you will likely get stuck here and never finish.

It's a huge accomplishment to actually finish a first draft of your story. The tendency of a beginner is to fall in love with it and lose objectivity. It's normal to look at the finished story as you would a newborn baby. It was conceived and carried in the womb of your soul for months until delivery. Now you think that everyone should love it as much as you do.

I like to tell beginning writers at this stage, "You have just fallen exhausted across the finish line after running a marathon. But I am telling you now to get up and run a 440." Some will simply not do it. Actually, I don't recommend that you begin as soon as you finish. Take another rest, and then run the 440. But at this stage you will have to ask yourself if you are really ready to publish, or if you should refine the manuscript some more. I recommend that you refine it. If you agree, this means that you don't just want to deliver a good story; you are ready to rewrite for excellence.

RISK AND REWARD

As a postscript to the magazine article I referenced in this chapter, it was published in *The Christian Outdoorsman's* inaugural issue as a featured article titled, "The Last Photograph." The title came from the defining scene. When the magazine was released, the article was sensational. People were deeply moved, and many sought me out as the author—often with moist eyes—to tell me how deeply the story had affected them. This was when I knew that God had indeed called this testimony from the manuscript of my life and was using it for His purposes.

Years later, after moving from Texas to Colorado, the story was expanded and published in a beautiful hardback from Thomas Nelson Publishers (Nashville, 1995). The book was also titled, *The Last Photograph*. The emotional responses to the book continued the pattern begun with the magazine article.

As I write today, the actual last photograph of Gordon sits framed on a shelf in my office, reminding me to always listen for God's voice and obey. I still receive emails and letters from people all over the world, expressing their appreciation for this book. I am aware of more lives touched and changed by this story than by any other I have written.

Your Public Story

But to get here you must push beyond your comfort zone. Without overcoming the writer's fear of rejection, rewards like this are not possible.

Chapter Three

WHAT MAKES A GOOD STORY GOOD?

What makes a good story good? There are many manifestations of the answer, but they all boil down to just three words: *a good storyteller*. What kind of storyteller are you?

My signature line for years has been: "Everyone has a story, and it's better than they think." But while this is true, not everyone has the skills to effectively tell his story. You may have a great story and yet be a poor storyteller. You may have a good story and know someone you trust who could make it better. Or, you may be approached by a professional who promises to make your story great—for a price. What will you choose?

I have heard many at this stage who quote Philippians 4:13—"I can do all things through Christ who strengthens me." They cite this scripture in order to insist that Christ qualifies them to write their own story. This is what I call "playing the God card." There is no way to argue against it. So, I say, "I'm here when you finish and will evaluate the manuscript if you'd like."

My experience with these "God card" manuscripts has run the gamut. Very few have won my praise. Most have earned a harsh review. It's painful for me to dash people's fantasies, but when they invest themselves in reaching an audience, it's better for me to tell the truth. I tell them that the Christ who strengthened them to write the first draft will also strengthen them to rewrite it. He will also strengthen them to decide if someone else would be a better storyteller in their place.

It's important to properly evaluate your own abilities. While it's true that you can do all things through Christ, God does not call you to do all things. He calls you to do certain things, and He sees you as part of a body that needs other members to be complete. If you are not the best storyteller for your story, ask God to guide you to the right one. Even so, finding a co-writer can be a daunting process.

FINDING A GOOD STORYTELLER

First of all, there are amateur writers who might volunteer to write your story. I never discount small beginnings. It is rare, but sometimes God has an emerging talent at just the right stage of development to give you an amazing manuscript. You will have to evaluate this person's abilities by asking to read other things he has written. Ask yourself if the style and approach fits your own. If so, I recommend that you have him write two or three sample chapters for you to evaluate. Do this with *zero obligation* to continue. In fact, you should write a small letter of agreement with the writer before he begins, making it clear that this is a writing test with no promise to continue.

Professional writers will vary in cost according to their experience. As in most transactions, you tend to get what you pay for. But not always. If you seek a professional, hire the best you can afford, but check out his reputation with other clients first. Some writers might agree to ghostwrite your book. That means they will write in your voice using first person and not have their name on the cover as a co-writer. Usually you pay extra for this kind of anonymity from an established writer.

Most co-writers will want their name to appear on the cover. Your name will appear in large print, and the co-writer will be listed as "with" followed by his name. A few years ago, I wrote the autobiography of Winfried Wentland, a special forces German soldier from Hamburg, Germany, who became Reinhard Bonnke's truck driver in Africa. It is a tale of travelling extreme back roads through war zones, demonic strongholds, and horrific atrocities, while facing corruption at every border crossing. The cover reads, "*By Life or by Death*, Winfried Wentland with Stephen Bransford." Listing the co-writer on the cover means that his reputation will be on the line based on the skills demonstrated in the book. In my case, I am definitely proud to have my name associated with Winfried's story. I recommend finding a co-writer who will likewise feel proud of your story.

If you choose to go with a co-writer, amateur or professional, you should write the full agreement in a contract. Never give up the copyright to your work. You normally pay the writer as a "work for hire," which means there will be no royalties paid or shared with the co-writer once the book is complete. If you cannot afford the writer of your choice, you can offer to share a portion of any net amounts you receive from selling the book as an incentive. You can go online and find good guidance regarding co-writer contracts and what should be included. Simply enter "writer collaboration agreements" in your search engine. But whatever you do, never proceed without a signed contract. Times change. People change. Your circumstances change. Writing a book is a marathon not a fifty-yard dash. You need a commitment that is equal to the task.

FINDING A GOOD EDITOR

An editor can help you or hurt you. Finding the right editor is something that has been good for me, and I recommend it. However, no editor at all is better than a bad one. So, what makes a good editor?

A good editor will not change your story or your style. You are the author, and your story is your property. It's good if it bears the stamp of your personality, even if it's not politically or academically correct. An editor must respect that. Editors can help with grammar, punctuation, usage, and style—up to the point of changing your content. A good editor will *suggest* improvements to your manuscript, even structural changes, but will never *dictate* them.

I readily admit that I am a storyteller first and will always err on the side of reaching my audience. If the *Chicago Manual of Style* gets in the way of a good yarn, I'll choose the story over being correct every time. I write for the common man, not for literary critics or college professors. I do not always use full sentences. Really. Sometimes I'll resort to slang. And I love clichés! They are *tried and true* and communicate so efficiently. I don't deliberately violate the accepted rules of creative writing schools or English composition classes, but I refuse to let them get in the way of my story. That's what I recommend for you.

So where can you find a good editor? You might begin by searching for a writers group in your area. Another source is the

What Makes a Good Story Good?

Christian Writers Market Guide. This resource is updated every year and will connect you to every aspect of the writing, publishing, and bookselling world. Other places to find an editor might be at writers conferences or online writing forums. These helps are readily available to you and simply require that you reach out and enter the world of professional writers.

AN AUTHENTIC VOICE

At Charis Bible College, I teach a course on techniques of fundraising letter writing. Years ago, I had a student who had come out of a redneck, drug-dealing lifestyle in the deep South. He had been seriously wounded in a gun battle and had subsequently invited Jesus into his life as Savior and Lord. In time, he had started a ministry outreach to other druggies, drug dealers, and street people. He had been writing a letter to a network of supporters and had raised enough money to buy a facility, and had run it for several years. But when he took my course, he suddenly felt embarrassed by his lack of formal education. He thought that he needed me to take his fundraising letters to a more respectable level, and he asked me to read a recent sample.

When I read his letter, I was totally arrested by the authenticity of his voice on the page. In a million years, I could never duplicate his redneck, Larry-the-Cable-Guy language and mannerisms. It rang so true to who he was in real life. That is the goal of all good communication. I told him that if I cleaned up his style I wouldn't do him any favors. His donors would sense something phony right away.

"If it ain't broke don't fix it," I told him. "Don't change a thing, and never feel embarrassed about the way you express yourself again. You help us feel the desperation of life on the mean streets where you live. And you show us the difference Christ makes. Keep up the good work."

I was able to see the value in this student's authentic voice because I'm not a person who cares so much about being technically correct. This is good, and sometimes not so good. It was good for this student's confidence as a storyteller, but it also means that sometimes I can hurt myself and not know it. Most good storytellers are like me in that regard. We have blind spots because we get a thrill from delivering a good story and are lost with the grammar, usage, punctuation, and spelling. So, when looking for help, you need to find the right balance. Your editor should be devoted to preserving your voice and your story first and foremost. Once you've found that person, let him comb through your work and suggest any corrections or changes that might improve it. Then choose which advice to follow as best you can. Remember, storytelling is not an absolute science. Nothing is perfect. So, trust your instincts in the final edit.

FINDING THE WRONG STORYTELLER

In the fall of 2009, Christopher and Deborah McDermott brought their two autistic boys to a meeting at Andrew Wommack's Bible College in Walsall, England. They were determined that Andrew pray for the healing of their sons. He did, and dramatic improvements began immediately.

What Makes a Good Story Good?

In the spring of 2010, I travelled to England with Andrew and met the McDermotts. They were elated to report that their boys were now normal, healthy children. By 2012, the medical authorities who had declared the boys incurable officially documented both of them free of all symptoms of autism. This was an outstanding miracle.

That year I travelled with my video stories team to the McDermotts' home to document how it all had happened. This became one of the most dynamic stories we had ever produced in a series of ministry videos called *Healing Journeys*.

After the story was seen worldwide on Andrew's daily TV broadcast, Deborah was suddenly in demand to minister to other parents coping with autism. She found herself repeating the same stories and advice so often it was wearing her out. After months of seeking ghostwriters in England, Deborah simply could not find a professional there who shared her faith. It was then that she asked if I would write their family story in a book that she could give to the desperate people who wanted the full details of her journey.

I was highly complimented. It was a story I very much wanted to write. I browsed the extensive journal she had written and realized that it would require more from me than I could deliver at the time. I had already contracted to write a book for another ministry, and between that obligation and my full-time position directing Andrew's television department, there was not enough of me left over to honor another commitment. In the meantime, I interviewed two ministry staff members who wanted to launch out as professional writers to see if one of them might be right for Deborah. The writing samples they supplied failed to win our confidence.

At last, in 2016, Deborah felt she had found the right co-writer in America. It was someone associated with another major television ministry that she really trusted. Perhaps she trusted too much. Signing a contract in May of that year, she and Christopher paid the writer a healthy advance to begin writing.

In June of 2017, they finally received a finished first draft and were terribly disappointed. Even worse, when they told the writer all of the changes they wanted to make in the book, the writer refused to do it, even though the contract contained rewrite provisions. Since the writer had violated the terms of the contract, they terminated the deal and walked away with a very bad taste in their mouths. Discouraged and beaten, Deborah wrote me that she simply could not bear to think about the book anymore. It looked like a sad ending to a very good story.

BECOMING THE RIGHT STORYTELLER

Six months later, however, the God who raises the dead spoke to Deborah's heart that she was to write the book herself, with her husband serving as editor. As she obeyed, inspiration hit her concerning content, structure, and style. It was as if the story was being downloaded. She finished in just a couple of weeks.

In the opening chapter, she set up the main conflict of her faith versus the prevailing wisdom of the medical establishment. The doctors insisted she "become friends with the incurable diagnosis of autism." She was told that to reject the label was to reject her own sons. Autism was who they *were*, the experts said. She should receive it as a gift from God. She knew this was wrong and began to declare that autism was the enemy. Following

What Makes a Good Story Good?

this dramatic opening chapter, she began telling her story in the form of a diary, tracing her life with her boys. In wrenching detail, she revealed the agonizing and amazing process of defeating autism through her relationship to God.

She sent the fresh manuscript to me as I was travelling in Africa with Andrew. I began reading on the plane and could not put it down. I recommended only a few changes to polish it up. It is self-published now and available on Amazon—*Autism Healed: One Woman's Fight to Save Her Sons* by Deborah McDermott. Looking at Amazon today, I see that her book has nothing but 5-star reviews!

This may seem like a tortuous path to a wonderful finish line. Deborah will agree with that, but she will also tell you that it was worth it. They might have skipped the part about paying the writer for such a disappointing draft, but then, maybe not. Who knows how we are prepared through disappointment and setbacks to be the instrument God uses when the time is right? Perhaps these trials became important motivators turning Deborah into the very best storyteller for her story.

Recently, I saw Christopher and Deborah at an Andrew Wommack Ministries healing conference. They had set up a booth to share their story with others, and they were all smiles. Their book had sold out. Deborah continues to travel and speak in Europe and America about her experience of successfully defying the medical establishment. Wherever she speaks, her book sells rapidly.

Perhaps, like Deborah, you feel that God is calling you to write your own story. What are the skills and techniques that will make you a good storyteller?

GOOD STORYTELLING

A good storyteller correctly assumes that no one automatically cares about what he has to say. It is his job to grab the attention of the readers and draw them into the story, helping them to care about it. To do this requires listening for the download from the Holy Spirit. But, having some basic understanding of human nature—and especially of human emotions—also helps. After all, when an audience cares about your story, it's an emotional response, not a cold decision.

Good storytelling begins with choosing a selling title. Ironically, the title is often the last choice that is made. After the story is completed, a theme appealing to the sensibilities of the audience is chosen. If a publisher is involved, the title will be chosen by the marketing team. It is their job to sell the book to the public, and they are only as good as their last bestseller.

In my experience, I like to choose what is called a working title when I begin to write. This title at the beginning may or may not make it to the final edit. To choose this working title, I first analyze the main theme of my story, and I stand it up against the mere subplots. This happens as I inventory my story elements. Then I project myself into the audience that does not care, and ask myself, *Is there a title that captures the main theme and arouses my curiosity to read the first page of this book?* That becomes my working title. So far, I'm pleased to say, my working titles have all been chosen by the publisher's marketing team at the end. But on certain challenging stories, I have changed working titles several times during the writing process before offering my final answer. Whatever the chosen title, it is always about reaching the audience.

Deborah McDermott's title and subtitle seem perfect: *Autism Healed: One Woman's Fight to Save Her Sons*. The main title arouses curiosity in the vast majority of people who believe autism is incurable. How can it be healed? The subtitle promises that this is the story of a fight. Anyone who knows someone with an autistic child will appreciate the truth in that statement. Deborah not only fought the disease but fought the prejudice of the medical world at the same time. This adds a huge weight to the conflict, and it is reflected in the title. *Autism Healed* is a mother's raging fight to save her boys from a living hell against all the odds. Her title is not false advertising.

STORYTELLERS AT PLAY

A good storyteller not only assumes that no one wants to hear what he has to say, he does not *resent* them for it. He knows that it is his job to capture their attention and help them care about what he cares about.

How does he do that? In a word, he doesn't just write; he plays. He takes his material and plays with it until something entertaining pops out. New words, phrases, examples, illustrations, insights, discoveries, parallels, poetry—the list is endless. He asks, *Does this change make the story better?* as he stacks, sorts, and maneuvers words on the page. As he works, he sees that his words are more than words. They are ideas, descriptions, actions, thoughts, insights, and feelings. He continues to play with how to position the intriguing stuff until the entire process takes on a life of its own. There are no shortcuts here. This kind of play will seem like work to the beginner, but it is precisely the work that mediocre writers fail to do.

This is where gifts of the Spirit will manifest for a communicator. When the gifts are active, work becomes play. *Play* is the right word. Some people don't realize that the Holy Spirit is playful. The first two fruits of the Spirit are love and joy, qualities that encourage freedom and play. At some point, a good storyteller at play senses that he is performing a work beyond himself. He has become an instrument in the hands of God, and the story that emerges bears heaven's fruit.

Once a writer or a storyteller in any medium has entered this zone, he can't go back. He craves to know it again and again. It becomes more important to him than a royalty check, fame, a career, publication, meeting a goal, a deadline, or winning an award for excellence.

This experience is actually available to anyone in any walk of life, not just writers and creative artists. God created mankind for relationship, for participation in His dance of eternal life. There is no end to the number of steps you can learn to become a better dance partner. These steps are marked by beauty, joy, freedom, and fulfillment. And they always make for better storytelling.

THE BONES OF A STORY

A good storyteller begins with a basic story structure in mind. Where would your body be without bones? It would be a formless mass of living tissue, unable to move or function. Bones are

What Makes a Good Story Good?

the structure that gives your body a shape, identity, and mobility. Likewise, every good story is fleshed out on a recognizable skeleton. So, what are the bones of a good story?

Chronology provides the most obvious structure. Every good story has a beginning, a middle, and an end. The storyteller arranges his story elements along a timeline. Once the timeline is complete, the writer knows where he is going and where he has come from. At some point he may change the chronology to make better sense of a sequence of events. For example, he may use flashback as I did in *The Last Photograph*. Some skillful writers are able to jump forward and backward in time, and jump from one main character to another. This is a technique that can work for the veteran writer, but is not recommended for the beginner.

In general, you should understand that using flashback is risky. By sticking with the timeline, the audience discovers things as you discover them. You are sharing a journey, and this is a very good thing. Flashback will give the audience some information that is normally discovered later in the story. It removes some of the intrigue and mystery. You must determine if the tradeoff is worth it for the reader. If you're wrong, you'll regret it.

IN MEDIAS RES

A good storyteller begins in the middle of action. Professional writers call this technique *In Medias Res*. This is a Latin term that means "in the middle of things." Too often, amateurs begin by writing *about* their story instead of writing the story. The best way to avoid this problem is to find a defining scene and start in the middle of the action. When I wrote my first novel about a circuit-riding preacher, *Riders of the Long Road*, it began like this:

"Silas!" Emily's scream pierced the boy's slumber. He lurched upward in the chair, eyes fluttering open. Who was Silas? he wondered, and why had his mother called for him? The anguish in her voice had started his heart pounding in his chest.

By starting in the middle of an action, I have intrigued the reader. I have set a scene without describing it. A boy is sleeping in a chair, not a bed. Why? He hears his mother scream an unfamiliar name. He is left with the sound of his beating heart. This all must be explained in the pages to come, but my readers have been arrested by an action that demands they keep reading.

Deborah McDermott used the same technique to begin *Autism Healed—One Woman's Fight to Save Her Sons*:

I can still hear her voice, so crisp and businesslike: "Mrs. McDermott, your son has autism. In fact, he has a form of it called Asperger's Syndrome."

She spoke with authority, as if she knew everything and I knew absolutely nothing. After all, she was the esteemed therapist and I was merely a physically and emotionally wrecked mother, my thoughts and opinions hardly worthy of consideration.

"You need to make friends with the diagnosis, Mrs. McDermott. I'm completely serious. You must make friends with it."

Make friends with it?

It?

What Makes a Good Story Good?

By choosing to begin her story in this scene, Deborah creates instant sympathy for herself as a "wrecked" mother. The main conflict of the entire book is seen on page one, as Deborah struggles against the dominant wisdom and authority of the therapist. By writing in first person, as well as using the device of a diary, Deborah draws the reader inside the drama of her battle. It is personal. Again, the reader is arrested and must continue reading to answer the questions raised.

INTERNAL DRAMA

A good storyteller takes the reader inside his characters, except when writing a screenplay. This was a lesson I learned the hard way.

I began my career writing for a Christian television network. After several years of creating fundraising films and dramatic commercials, I managed to write my first screenplay, titled, *Riders of the Long Road*. Screenplays are written to be read by producers, directors, actors, costumers, casting directors, and such. My experience in writing for television production had caused me to feel comfortable writing to this audience. However, I had a painful wake-up call when I attempted to turn that first screenplay into a novel.

The wake-up call came in the form of a rejection letter from my editor at Doubleday. After seven months of writing and reaching the brink of exhaustion, he told me that my manuscript was not publishable. It was a devastating blow. He explained that I had failed to understand the basic difference between writing a screenplay and a novel.

"Screenplays are about what people say and do," he said. "Novels are about what they think and feel. You have to take your audience inside your characters."

Alas, I had described a story full of dramatic word pictures and actions that gave a professional actor or director all they needed to interpret the characters, but I had failed to write out the inner drama for the reading audience of amateurs. In truth, I had imagined that my writing style was clever and trendsetting. Boy, was I wrong!

Having just fallen exhausted across the finish line of a marathon, I was now required to get up and run the 440! The editor told me I had just two weeks to fix everything or they would terminate my contract. Very soon, I realized the deadline was beyond my reach, but I am happy to say that it was not beyond God's reach. Sometimes a dream has to die to be resurrected. I met the deadline and completed an award-winning novel in just seven miraculous days. The full story of how that happened is available through a blog on my website titled, "Award Winning Mom."

The lesson is clear: People who read books, whether novels or nonfiction, need the writer to take them by the hand and write the thoughts and feelings of the characters throughout the story.

AN ELEMENT OF SURPRISE

A good storyteller sees things other people miss. This creates an element of surprise throughout the narrative. These surprises are not necessarily shocking or bizarre. In most cases, they are simply amusing and informative ways of describing something ordinary. The reader's assumptions are constantly challenged with new ways of seeing his familiar world. He feels that he is going someplace worthwhile, discovering things he would otherwise not notice. When this happens, it gives the reader the sense that he is in the hands of a master storyteller.

How is this ability to surprise developed? In most cases, I would say the ability is a gift more than a skill. Over the years, I have cultivated a number of beginning writers who have excelled at this. I have also guided some who have failed to distinguish themselves. The difference seems to be in the predisposition of the writer.

With few exceptions, I have found the better storytellers are people who have experienced life in some extreme. Perhaps it is childhood trauma, abuse, war, religious oppression, divorce, abrupt family moves, international exposure, or a combination thereof. Of course, none of these things qualifies a good storyteller in and of itself, but it often causes the writer to see things from a unique point of view, and this is a valuable asset. Seeing things from outside the mainstream frequently adds an entertaining element to any message.

The downside is that very creative and unorthodox people can make others they work with feel uncomfortable. I must say that I have protected and championed "problem" employees over the years because I have been very willing to risk corporate disapproval in order to cultivate an exceptional storyteller. Sometimes this has worked to everyone's advantage, and other times it has backfired. Sadly, I have had to terminate people I would otherwise support because of their nonconformity to a corporate culture.

I bring this up because when you're shopping for a good storyteller, you need to be prepared to accommodate someone who is a bit out of the box. If you feel totally comfortable and safe with a writer, you may be putting your audience to sleep.

Finally, if you are looking in your own mirror for a good storyteller, you need to be brutally honest. Ask yourself if you have looked at your story for so long that you no longer see the forest for the trees. If so, your descriptions may fall far short of their potential to capture and hold an audience. Find a good storyteller. A good storyteller sees things other people miss.

SETUP AND PAYOFF

A good storyteller uses setup and payoff throughout his story. This is a technique that separates really good writers from the mundane. In order to accomplish it well, the writer needs to plan ahead. He anticipates great moments in his story and plants a detail early in the manuscript that will set up the reader to appreciate its deeper meaning later when the moment occurs.

I have found that I don't always plan properly in advance. As I rewrite and polish the story, it occurs to me how I can go back and plant better details early in the writing to enhance a moment of revelation. Also, as I write, I often receive an illumination about a moment in the story that was not in my original story inventory. These are the most exciting events for me as a writer. They come from beyond my careful planning and indicate the work of the Holy Spirit.

What Makes a Good Story Good?

THE BOTTOM LINE

The ultimate setup and payoff for any story is what I call the bottom line. Is there a statement that is going to put the finishing touch on your story? That is the idea you want to set up during the entire story. When you come to the end of the story, you should unload the bottom line, and it should seem natural and relieve all the tension you have created. You want your readers to nod in agreement and say to themselves, "Of course!"

In *The Last Photograph*, I discovered the perfect bottom line as I dealt with extreme pain and guilt at my brother's unexpected death. My comfort came when the Lord reminded me that I had obeyed His voice and had used my camera to stop the competition and give my brother his place. Not knowing that he would not be with us for long, that obedience had allowed me to celebrate his life while he still lived. The bottom line is set up through the entire story and only revealed on the last page: "No unfinished business."

No unfinished business.

Today, I still grieve. I miss the phone calls, Gordon's arrogant laugh, his willpower. I miss trading manuscripts and stories, his talent, the articles and books he would have written, making a name for himself and his outfit. I miss the improvement he would have brought to my own writing. The horseback adventures, hunting, and fishing we would have shared. I miss the father and husband he was, and was still becoming. Most of all, I miss that great heart of his, that had only just begun to emerge from behind that outlaw beard. These are death's realities—things we cannot fully reconcile.

But I have a special comfort. I have the last photograph of Gordon. I share it with family and with friends who visit my home now located in the Rocky Mountains. I tell them about hearing the voice. I say, "I don't always hear it, but I pray that I will."

I do pray that I will.

LEAVE THEM WANTING MORE

After delivering the bottom line, it's time to stop writing. I am always amazed at the insecurity that shows up at the end of a story. There is always more that can be said, but it is best when the writer says to himself, "Enough said." I have read many stories in which the writer does not know how to bring everything in for a landing. One ending is added to another, which weakens the reader's sense of shared closure at the end of a book.

I think it's natural to overwrite the ending, but that is where a good editor can be helpful. Evaluate all your endings and choose one. Just one. This will be the one that depicts your bottom line. Restraining your urge to keep writing will serve your story well. A good storyteller knows that the best and most memorable stories leave the audience wanting more.

And that's what makes a good story good.

Chapter Four

WHAT MAKES A GOOD STORY BAD?

The voice on the phone lit me up like a shot of adrenaline. I was a starving artist who had made a promising start as a twice-published novelist. But my wife and I now shared a Colorado mountain cabin with a friend because the monthly rent was too much for my meager royalties. Every morning I would awaken and push myself to the word processor, believing that my big break was just around the corner.

On this morning, my agent was calling. Now, this was not just any agent. This man had negotiated multimillion-dollar contracts for some of the biggest authors in the business. And after reading my first two novels, he believed in me. Whenever he called, my pulse raced like a thoroughbred in the starting gate.

The telephone conversation did not disappoint. He wanted me to fly to Washington D.C., where I would meet a representative from a top publishing firm. I was being asked to interview a man whose life story had become a *New York Times* bestseller. The client wanted to write another book and needed to find a new co-author. I couldn't help myself. I began to fantasize fame and fortune.

Because of the success of the client's life story, his name had become a household word, but I had never read his book. That day I visited a bookstore and brought his bestseller home, devouring it from cover to cover. This was my cram course in breaking out of obscurity.

The story was a nonstop sequence of high adventure, intrigue, rescues, and thrills. The skillful writing revealed the inner workings of a minister and his mission in a way that made me laugh, cry, and pump my fist at the end. No wonder it had been a bestseller. This kind of excellent writing, of course, set the bar very high for me.

In the back of my mind grew a nagging question: Why did the client want to change horses in the middle of the stream? Why did he want a new co-writer? I had lived long enough to know that I would be measured against the success of the first book, not to mention the storytelling excellence that had brought it to the world.

BELIEVING THE HYPE

When I finally met the client, I felt that I was shaking hands with a legend. He was a man of action more than words. He had committed himself to a life of dangerous humanitarian work. His story inspired because of the risks he dared to take in serving God. I felt sure that I was about to hear more nail-biting episodes than I could possibly imagine. The key to my success, I believed, would be that the client had lived an even more adventurous life since the original work was written, and I would be the one to tell those new stories.

Across three days of interviewing, however, my preconceived notions began to fall apart. I saw the first red flag when he showed me the outline he wanted for the book. I paused to read it and felt as if my thoroughbred starting gate had just turned into a paddock.

As it turned out, he had a lot of stuff he was determined to tell the world now that he was famous—hard truths that they would rather ignore, challenges he thought his fans needed to accept, confrontations with their faithless timidity compared to his own heroic actions. He believed these inferior believers had made themselves a laughing stock to the world. The book he wanted to write would shame them into becoming better Christians. Or so he hoped.

I prayed that I could finesse his outline into something better. The motivation of shame had never produced quality results in my experience. Quite the opposite, in fact. The only people Jesus shamed in the Gospels were the religious folk who considered their performance to be miles above the rabble.

His outline totally departed from the success of the first book. In his bestseller, he had been the hero facing extraordinary challenges. It had been left to the Holy Spirit to call readers to a similar commitment. As it turned out—predictably—they had been content to stay at home, cheering him on like an army of couch potatoes, and frankly, this had chapped his holy hide.

By contrast, in the outline for the sequel, he seemed bent on demanding that his readers get off the couch and onto the playing field, ready or not. I put myself in the place of the reader, and there was simply no bait on the hook, no art in the message. He was shaming, challenging, and lecturing his adoring fans, something akin to cutting off the bestselling limb he was standing on.

In the kindest way possible, I told him that I would like to insert entertainment value into his outline. We needed to do more than tell people how the cow ate the cabbage. We needed to package his points in stories to help readers know what was at stake. We should explain that there is only one hero in the Gospel, and that is Christ alone. He enables the weakest among us to be strong. He supplies the power of the Holy Spirit when our life is on the line. I told him that we should begin on common ground with his readers and draw them confidently inside his world of risk and courage. That way, those who were at ease in Zion could feel the importance of rising to the challenge—even if they chose not to.

He fell ominously silent. He seemed bothered by the suggestion. This was not a good sign.

Finally, he said that there were too many seeker-friendly preachers out there dumbing down the Gospel for weak-minded Christians. He didn't want to be another one, playing down the self-sacrifice involved in following Jesus. It was time for flabby believers to take up their cross. He was a man to tell the truth and let the chips fall where they may.

I had to admire his gumption. But I did not feel called by God to spread gumption. As a follower of heaven's one true hero, I felt called to spread the good news that God's power is a gift, not a reward for courage. The same Lord who told us to carry our cross also promised that His yoke is easy and His burden light. God's Word reveals that our accomplishments are produced by the Spirit, not the flesh. It's about willingness, not will power. It's about bearing fruit, not producing a bumper crop of artificial holiness.

What Makes a Good Story Bad?

My challenge would be to help my client see that what I proposed would not dumb down the Gospel. Rather, it would make it accessible and unavoidable to the audience he wanted to reach. Rather than intimidate, belittle, and discourage his readers, it would inspire and engage them so that more readers would be enticed to consider the hard challenges he presented.

Unfortunately, over the course of the next weeks and months I failed to make my case. He remained firmly planted in his determination to make a very good story bad. Eventually, we agreed to part ways, and my vision of fame and fortune vanished with him.

DESPISING THE AUDIENCE

Over the course of my career, I have been asked to serve as a professional storyteller for a number of clients. Some of our collaborations have been successful; others, disastrous. As I sort my list of failures, I find three kinds of thinking that guarantee a good story will go bad:

1. Despising the audience
2. Demanding truth, the whole truth, and nothing but the truth
3. Preaching to the choir

The first involves the story I just related about the bestselling author. When the storyteller is filled with the things he wants to say and ignores what the audience is able and ready to hear, he is despising the audience, and a good story goes bad.

We sometimes call this too much information, or TMI for short, but it is much more than that. It is a form of self-centeredness. The over-full storyteller is too proud of his material. Too close to it. He takes himself too seriously. He loses perspective, he loses his sense of humor, and he loses the ability to bring the dead elements of his story to life for the reader.

The things the over-stuffed storyteller wants to say need to be broken down into bite-sized wisdom the audience can swallow. And each bite needs the proverbial spoonful of sugar. This requires lowering the author's grandiose fantasies about himself and embracing compassion for the reader. To do that, he must project himself into the reader's point of view. This requires a work of the imagination. Good storytellers empathize. They can see, hear, touch, smell, and feel in someone else's shoes.

DEMANDING TRUTH

When a storyteller insists on telling the truth, the whole truth, and nothing but the truth, a good story goes bad. Notice a subtle difference here: Truth is truth, whether you demand it or not. In storytelling it is the *demand* for truth that gets in the way of ministry, not the truth itself.

Every story should be true, but a story that insists on being absolute "truth" is self-deceived. A good storyteller knows the difference and knows how to discover and share what is true and valuable without claiming to express the entire truth of the matter. As the Apostle Paul cautioned, "We know in part, we prophesy in part."

My father was a preacher, and throughout my career I've been privileged to work with some amazing preachers, teachers,

What Makes a Good Story Bad?

and evangelists. I have studied their style and their delivery to be able to write in their voices. In every case, I have been amazed at the things they *don't* say. In this age of high-decibel passion, the best communicators operate with surprising restraint. Always, they are thinking of how to best reach their audience, and they avoid unloading everything they know.

For example, I have seen that good speakers will tell the same story over and over again, but each time it is different. Certain details are included in one telling and left out of another. Why? Because the Holy Spirit quickens the minister to the needs of the audience at hand, and the speaker adapts the story to meet their need. The story is true each time, but it is not the whole truth. Nor should it be.

Storytelling involves deciding where to begin, what to leave out, and what to include in order to take the audience to a place of value. Often, amateur storytellers reject good technique because it is "not exactly the way things happened."

I have interviewed clients who have insisted that they want their story to be an exact photograph of what took place. While a good storyteller is able to create an excellent word picture, a word picture is not a photograph. If an exact photograph is what a client demands, I tell them they should hire a photographer. Even then, they are lying to themselves to think that what they produce is exactly "the way it happened." In truth, they have edited and fudged the details in a variety of ways just to get the facts to fit the size of the page or the limits of the article, book, documentary, or sermon. And when they are driven by a need to be absolutely exact, they usually adapt the material badly.

Good storytellers illuminate partial truth in a world of imperfect memory by the unction of the Spirit. This humbles the impulse to confine storytelling to the truth, the whole truth, and nothing but the truth. This kind of truth telling is sworn into court testimony, and it seldom reveals the truth—and never the whole truth. Besides, *it's boring.*

Good storytellers look at the bigger picture. They know that a true and good story is an impressionistic painting, not a photograph, and never a court document.

PREACHING TO THE CHOIR

When a storyteller tells what happened, and then tells what happened next, and next, and next, a good story goes bad.

This kind of storytelling is simple chronology: telling how one thing happened after another. And it's the most common entertainment killer on the planet. I see this so much from first-time storytellers, that it's almost predictable. In fact, that's how I started before I learned better.

This kind of storyteller is related to the truth-demanding storyteller but is more innocent and naïve. This is the kind of storytelling done at family gatherings, between best friends, in schools, or in church communities. It's the enthusiastic telling of what happened on your mission trip, retreat, vacation, or on the best or worst day of your life. Everyone in your audience is eager to hear what you have to say because they already know you and love you, and they vicariously participate in every word from your mouth. They share your enthusiasm and wish you only the best.

What Makes a Good Story Bad?

In essence, you are telling them what they want to hear, and they make you feel like a creative genius for doing it. This is a lethal combination when it comes to good storytelling.

We learn to tell this kind of story at the time we learn to talk. As we toddle about the house and stuff happens to us, or we do stuff, each incident becomes a story told to adoring parents. We can do no wrong.

The killer in this kind of storytelling is that it limits the audience to your friends and family. It's preaching to the choir. It suffers the same fate as the inside joke. Those on the inside laugh so hard they cry, but told to a new audience, it falls horribly flat. Let me assure you, beyond family and friends, no one cares about the stuff you do and the stuff that happens to you.

In the world of professional writers, we call this kind of storytelling episodic. You simply tell what happened or what you did. One episode is followed by another: *"And then we got off the bus... and then we went to the beach... and then we did some street evangelism... and it was awesome!"* Each episode is self-contained. It can be entertaining in itself, but it is not related in a meaningful way to the episode that precedes it, nor the one that follows. One incident simply follows another. *Yawn!*

To fix an episodic story you must rewrite without mercy. You must create a story arc and kill all the rabbit trails that depart from the spine of the story. You cannot spare a single episode, no matter how much your wife or mother loves it!

If you're telling an episodic story, you probably have no idea what a story arc is. As I explained in an earlier chapter, a story arc is the thread that ties all the episodes together. It is not just the story. It is what the story is about, what it means. It is bigger than any episode. It should be bigger than all of the episodes put together. It is the reason anything is told at all. An arc is like a bridge. It takes you from one place to another. It does this through a series of related events, or steps. The story arc must be something that people who don't know you or like you would be interested in following. It must be a journey we all want to take for our own good. This eliminates just about everything your friends and family ever heard from you.

Storytellers who remain amateur indulge themselves in the praises of a familiar audience. They do not accept the challenge of winning an indifferent audience, or even a hostile one. They become like the bad auditions collected by the *American Idol* TV series. Each singer is amazingly bad but doesn't know it because his friends and family have told him he's the next Elvis Presley. Episodic storytelling might get you to the audition, but never to Hollywood.

And that's what makes a good story bad.

Chapter Five

PUBLISHING STRATEGY

Your manuscript is complete, edited, and polished. You have written a good story. It may be fiction or nonfiction. Now what? Where and how do you get it published?

First, a word about your manuscript: Be sure to add a copyright notice at the bottom of the first page. It should read "copyright © (year) by (your name)." You might add the phrase, "All rights reserved." This is sufficient to protect your work and announce to professionals that it is a property that you own with rights attached to it that may be optioned and licensed in various ways.

When a legitimate publisher offers a contract for your work, they will name the rights they are licensing, and will spell out exactly how and when those rights can return to you as the copyright holder. Rights can be licensed again and again. They can be made exclusive or nonexclusive. All of these details are valuable and negotiable.

This is important: Never, ever sell or sign over your copyright to anyone at any time for any reason. No one knows the future value of your property, and many things can happen to increase its value as time passes and the world changes. Think of it as owning a vacant lot. If a shopping mall is built next door, and the owners need to lease or purchase your lot for parking, its value rises. Who knew?

Every writer's dream is to have an established publisher license the rights to publish his book. Mainstream publishers often pay the author an advance for writing the book, then they pay for printing, binding, and promoting it through their catalog and other distribution networks. It goes to bookstores, book clubs, e-book stores, and libraries. Their publicity department will seek reviews of your book in major journals. They will book you for public speaking and media interviews. As sales pile up, you will receive royalty checks. It can be a heady experience.

I achieved that dream with my first novel, *Riders of the Long Road*, published by Doubleday. We were reviewed in *The New York Times, Publisher's Weekly, Library Journal*, and many other media outlets nationwide. It sold 40,000 hardbacks, two book clubs, and made the bestseller list in the *Dallas Times Herald*. But there is a secret behind my success that I will share in this chapter—and you may not *like* what you learn. Dreams are necessary, but ultimately, reality prevails in the publishing world.

That's why I'm going to recommend today that you self-publish. There are many ways for you to do this, and I will return to the topic. But in the beginning, it's best that you face the truth: Getting an established publisher to pay an advance, print, promote, and distribute your book is a long shot. Check out this

Merriam-Webster definition of a long shot: "a venture involving great risk but promising a great reward if successful also: a venture unlikely to succeed."

CHASING THE LONG SHOT

In 2015, Andrew Wommack Ministries produced the *Healing Journey* of Nichole Marbach as a video testimony. She had been a church-going wife and mother in Chicago, who was diagnosed as bipolar with complications from childhood sexual abuse. Her condition deteriorated so badly, she became alcoholic, began secretly cutting herself, and was committed to mental hospitals repeatedly. Exhausting every therapy known to man, she was told that she was incurable and would simply have to cope for the rest of her life. But she began to discover truths in God's Word that set her mind and emotions free, and today she is a licensed minister, who speaks at churches and women's conferences. She graduated from Charis Bible College in Chicago and began to operate the Hope Center in Bolingbrook, Illinois.

When Nichole's *Healing Journey* aired on Andrew's daily television program, demand for her as a speaker grew worldwide. In February of 2016, she wrote to me about publishing her life story. She felt urged by God to write it—and had been doing so for months—and requested an editor. I connected her to a trusted editor and advised her to self-publish.

She labored for the next two years and finally completed a manuscript that she sent to me for evaluation. I found the descriptions of abuse and disorder to be vivid and dramatic, and the writing to be very good, but I felt that she had not described the process of change well enough. Her transformation felt almost magical, and I knew that it was a process with discouraging setbacks. I also felt that the book became "preachy" at the end. While preaching is not a ministry problem, as Nichole ministers to hurting people through preaching, it was a departure from the pure storytelling approach she had established throughout the narrative. I wanted her testimony to have artistic integrity.

Understandably, these criticisms seemed harsh. She was excited to have finished and had hoped that the writing process was complete. I sympathized, having been in her shoes a few times. This is true for all authors. Once our "baby" is born, through much labor, we long to hear that the whole world loves it as much as we do.

I told her that, in fact, she had written a good book, and more work was optional. The real question for her to ask herself was if she had finished what God had called her to do. If so, then I encouraged her to go forward and let the chips fall where they may. To her credit, she regrouped with her editor and addressed my concerns, emerging with a more polished manuscript in March of 2018. She was able to deliver twenty-one chapters of storytelling that preserved the artistic integrity of her testimony. But as a minister, she could not ignore the hurting people who she knew would be motivated by her story. For them, she added a section of ministry epilogs, which was a perfect solution.

She titled the book *Hold On to Hope*. As she began to let others read it, the manuscript brought universal praise. This

Publishing Strategy

was so nice for her to hear, especially after working through my earlier criticism.

In April of 2018, however, she fell under the spell of an author's agent. She gave him a copy of the manuscript, and he didn't just like it, he went bonkers for it. He said that a lot of people had good stories, but 99 percent of them couldn't produce a well-written page turner like hers. He told her that major secular publishers were suddenly hot after Christian books. His agency had already placed bestsellers for Joseph Prince, Joel Osteen, and Joyce Meyer. He felt sure the same publishers would compete with each other in order to offer her a very nice contract. The agent promised that the book proposal, which he would help her write, would be presented to the top five publishers in the world, and they would soon be knocking on her door.

Needless to say, this news sent Nichole into near ecstasy. The two-year process of writing the book had been far more tortuous than she had imagined. After all the hard work, it appeared that God was not just smiling on her, He was promoting her to the very top.

When she emailed me with the good news, I couldn't bring myself to dampen her spirits. Besides, I'm not always right about things. Maybe my self-publishing advice had not been the best solution for her after all. I congratulated her, hoping against hope that her book would hit the big time, and her dream would come true.

CELEBRITY SELLS

As time passed, however, another reality began to set in. One by one, the big five publishing houses declined her book. She was hurt and stunned to silence. At that point, the agent told her not to be discouraged. He switched his approach to some of the top evangelical publishers, sure that they would want the book: Tyndale, Baker Books, Thomas Nelson, Crossway, and the like. One by one, they also declined. Finally, an approach was made to Charismatic publishing houses, which were theologically sympathetic to the miraculous content of her story. They declined.

The final rejection email from a publisher was worded this way: *"I think Nichole's passion, ministry, and testimony are amazing. If it was up to me, I would LOVE to partner with her in the production of the book, but I don't know that a straight testimony book would do well for us sales-wise. I wish that were not the case, but the market is not easy for autobiographical life testimonies."*

It was now October of 2018, and Nichole wrote to me of her deep discouragement: *"...I have to admit I am pretty disappointed and feel like I keep getting teased over and over then let down. I am tempted to not publish my story at all anymore after this... The hardest part is when they told me in the beginning, they thought I would have four to five contracts within a couple of weeks and instead I have received only rejections. I would have preferred to self-publish rather than have my story rejected over and over again by every publisher. Having to have some real conversations with the Father over this one."* In another email she commented:

"... I am a no name and I guess that is part of the problem. I am not a nothing in the kingdom of God though."

I could not agree with Nichole more about that last statement, and that is the main point of this book. I will return and expand on the idea, but for now, here is a hard reality: If you are not famous, your biography will not be published by a mainstream publisher no matter how compelling it is. If Nichole's excellent book *Hold On to Hope* had been written by Joel Osteen, Joyce Meyer, or Joseph Prince, it would have become a bestseller. They have worldwide television audiences who see them regularly. Celebrity sells.

BECOMING A CELEBRITY

I first encountered this reality on April 27, 1985, when I received the Texas Literary Festival award for fiction for my first novel. Before the ceremony, heiress, socialite, and fashion designer, Gloria Vanderbilt, and I sat at adjacent book tables at the back of the Anatole ballroom in Dallas, Texas. Gloria was the keynote speaker and the main draw for the event. She had just published her autobiography, *Once Upon a Time*. Our publishers had piled both of our tables high with hardbacks, anticipating big sales from the crowd.

As I sat there, I watched people walk past me with only a glance. No one bought a single one of my books. At the same time, they were lined up around the room to have Gloria Vanderbilt autograph *Once Upon a Time*. Some were holding multiple copies of the book. I began to realize that people hunger to know intimate details about someone who is famous. It is woven into the human genome.

As the line of people slowly passed in front of me, I sank deeper into my chair. What could I do? There was simply no way that I would jump up and start hawking my book like a carnival barker: *"Hey, you people don't know what you're missing! Here's an exciting story that's really worth reading. Just $16.95, get a copy of this historical novel while supplies last!"* No. I just couldn't go there. Rather, I felt like disappearing, embarrassed to learn that nobody cared about my award-winning baby.

What happened next became the biggest lesson I learned that night. In my acceptance speech, I said this: "Tonight, in her speech, Gloria Vanderbilt told us that families deal us our greatest wounds in life. I agree with her. But the story in my book is built around the idea that it is God's pleasure to use families to also provide our greatest healing."

Then I referenced my father, who was seated in the crowd, as the inspiration behind the character of Silas Will in *Riders of the Long Road*. I told them that Dad was serving as a modern-day circuit-riding preacher in Alaska, visiting eighty churches via bush pilot. When I had him stand, the room gave him a warm ovation.

At the end of my speech, Gloria stood on the dais and tearfully embraced me. She autographed a copy of *Once Upon a Time* (which I have to this day) and asked for an autographed copy of *Riders of the Long Road*. She left by a private celebrity entrance, and I returned to my book table to sign autographs for the rest of the evening until every one of my books was sold.

What changed? I was no longer an unknown. The people in that room could suddenly relate to me and my family story. I became a celebrity, at least for one night. I was already an award-winning author. So what? My speech about Silas and Dad, plus Gloria's hug, made everyone in the room want a piece of me. When you connect with an audience, your books will sell.

Celebrity sells. This may sound hard and cynical, but it is not. In fact, this is clearly one of the most important ideas in this book. Celebrity is something you must learn to cultivate and master as an author. Who are you? What kind of celebrity are you? Do you know a celebrity who will endorse you? How will you connect with people?

HARD REALITIES

With the odds so against a contract from a mainstream publisher, you may wonder how I was able to get *Riders of the Long Road* published by Doubleday in the first place. Good question. First of all, no one in the publishing world cared that I was a good or bad writer. When I first called the editor at Doubleday, I told him that I had written a screenplay that had been optioned by a New York movie company, and I would like to turn it into a novel. I let him know that the movie company was the one that had just produced the mega-hit *Superman* with Christopher Reeve. (Celebrity not only sells, it opens doors.)

In that first conversation, I was told that the day my movie went into production they would send me a contract for the novelization rights. The editor explained that I was an unknown author with no track record of success. The movie, however, would most likely promote enough book sales so that they would at least break even. The movie amounted to a lot of free publicity that would translate into book sales. That was the basis of their verbal offer. It was a cold, hard business decision having nothing to do with my passion for the story.

As months went by, I refrained from putting all my eggs in the Doubleday basket. I called several other publishers and made the same pitch. Every one of them gave me the same answer. With a movie deal, I had a choice of publishers.

This opened my eyes. A year later, the motion picture failed to go into production, and all the rights that had been optioned by the movie company returned to me, the copyright owner. If I wanted to get a publishing deal at this stage, I would have to find a new business proposition.

In fact, during that same year, I had obtained the endorsement of the Bicentennial Commission of the United Methodist Church. Francis Asbury, the original circuit-riding preacher, was a Methodist icon. A statue of him on horseback stood in Washington D.C. bearing the inscription, "The Prophet of the Long Road," a phrase that had influenced my title. I knew that the Methodist endorsement was my best opportunity to get *Riders of the Long Road* published as a novel, but I had to hone my pitch so that the publisher wouldn't miss its significance. I did my homework and decided that I would lead with some impressive numbers.

I called Doubleday and told the editor that soon 12.5 million American Methodists would celebrate their bicentennial and that

I had obtained their endorsement for *Riders of the Long Road*. I suggested that Doubleday would do well to publish the novel in spite of the failure of the movie deal.

Once they confirmed my claim with the Methodist Bicentennial Committee, they agreed and sent me a contract. This meant that they took no risk on me. If I failed to write a competent adaptation of the screenplay, they would hire a ghostwriter to do it for me. The Methodists would promote the novel to an interested audience of 12.5 million members. With that endorsement Doubleday might actually make a profit in book sales without putting out any effort. Publishing is a business, and every publisher is trying to eliminate the odds of failure.

CHRISTIAN PUBLISHING

When it comes to Christian publishers, the same rules apply. They will look at your manuscript for its storytelling excellence, but they won't make a decision based on good writing and ministry value alone. The possible exception is if you have written a compelling Christian novel that fits one of their successful fiction genres: Romance, Historical, Thriller, or Crime. They see tons of really bad fiction. Well-written fiction stands out from the bad. Editors have a weakness for it. It is the ultimate long shot in publishing. They secretly wish they could do it themselves and will sometimes take a risk when they see real talent. Sometimes, however, means seldom—*almost never*.

Whether fiction or nonfiction, publishers want to know how many books you can sell for them. Yes, you thought the publisher would sell your book for you, right? Nah. With an unknown author, it's the other way around. Celebrity sells, and they want to know what kind of celebrity you are. They want to know who knows you. Who wants to read something you wrote simply because you wrote it?

They will ask you how many books you have already published. How many of your books have sold? How many times a year do you engage in public speaking? How many people are present at each event? How often do you do radio? TV? Can you open the door to a *Fox and Friends* interview? TBN? *700 Club?* James Robison? Jim Bakker? Other media? Do you have a website? How much traffic does it see? How many followers do you have on social media? Do you have a ministry? How big is your mailing list? How many active donors are on your list?

In other words, they are asking you to do all the heavy lifting for them in terms of book sales. I was able to do that for Doubleday with the Methodist endorsement. All publishers are looking for numbers to reduce their risk. Hard numbers, not wild speculations. If you cannot produce hard numbers, you will join their list of long shots and begin your collection of rejection letters.

This can be the end of the line for you and your dream of being published by a mainstream publisher. But I say the end is just the beginning. I agree completely with Nichole when she says, *"I am a no name and I guess that is part of the problem. I am not a nothing in the kingdom of God though."* Amen, Nichole. You have a story, and it's better than you think, and you live in a time of unprecedented opportunity to reach your audience through self-publishing.

SELF-PUBLISHING

Self-publishing used to be a despised option, but those days are gone. Long gone. There is no stigma anymore. Thousands of authors are making significant book sales and substantial incomes without the benefit of a mainstream publishing company. The margin of profit the author receives on each book sold through self-publishing is vastly greater than the pittance that mainstream publishers pay. This means that selling fewer self-published copies will bring a greater return to the author.

In the old days, like fifteen years ago, major publishers were the only legitimate game in town. They were financially strong enough to print and hold an anticipated inventory of books for sale. If sales were not sufficient, they would dump the remaining inventory into the aftermarket at bargain-basement prices to reduce their losses. This happened to three of my novels at the end of their first printing. I receive nothing from the aftermarket sales.

Years ago, this situation was a huge challenge to self-publishers. Printing costs, inventory storage, distribution costs, shipping, and buy-backs on returned books were enough to sink the ship of any self-published author. I know. It sank my first self-publishing enterprise in the 1990s. But everything changed with the development of digital production, digital distribution, and digital marketing. The costs are now within reach of every serious writer, plus the development of on-demand printing and e-book sales make it possible for an author to publish and reach an audience for very little, and in some cases, for nothing.

Helpful software and publishing tools are readily and reasonably available. Beyond that, we have low-cost to no-cost options for making books through Kindle Direct Publishing (found at kpd.amazon.com), plus excellent services, such as Lulu.com, BookBaby.com, and others. None of this was in existence when I self-published in the '90s. I couldn't even imagine it.

Typesetting, book cover design, interior design, ISBN bar coding, e-book distribution, hard- and soft-back printing on demand—it's all there for you. You'll have to shop and find the right combination, but you are surrounded with solutions. I won't try to sort through the information available, but I will just say, as I wrote this paragraph, I simply put into my search engine "best self-publishing options" and found everything you need to know about publishing your story. Go there, and follow the instructions. It's a no-brainer.

However, if you feel overwhelmed by it all, if you have absolutely no capacity to navigate this brave new world of self-publishing, if everything is just Greek to you, you will need to find help. Who has God placed in your life that is gifted at the things you are not? Start shopping, and be prepared to pay them for their expertise. Don't expect people to donate their services. Some people will offer to do that, but when something is free, no one is obligated. You usually get what you pay for. But don't just throw money at it. Don't give away the store. Negotiate a level of payment you are comfortable with, and write your own letter of agreement to the terms. You don't need a lawyer. You can find templates for letters of agreement readily on the internet. The deal you make should be a win-win for both parties.

Publishing Strategy

STARTING WITH ZERO

If you simply have no financial resources, you can make "back-end" agreements with your collaborators. This means that you write an agreement promising that when books sell you will pay a modest percentage of your royalties or profits to each person who has helped you get published. These might include the cover designer, the proofreader, the interior book designer, the online technical coordinator who helps you with Kindle-Amazon, Lulu, or BookBaby. The percentage given to each of these helpers is completely negotiable and up to you. What you need are friends who share your passion for your story so much that they are willing to take the risk with you. Perhaps you will find these folks where you attend church.

This is part of understanding who you are. Have you been a good steward of the friends and family God has placed in your life? They are your best way forward. If you have turned friends and family into enemies, don't blame them. Look at yourself before God and ask Him how to repair the damage. But be careful here. If suddenly you are currying favor with antagonists and asking them to invest in your dream, good luck with that. People want to be appreciated, not used.

Be honest with them. You can speculate about the potential for returning a profit, but make sure they know that you cannot promise a return. Not even major publishers can promise that. They do everything they can to increase the odds of being successful, but most of their ventures fail. Big bestsellers fund a lot of trial and error for publishing houses. It is a long shot for everyone.

Over the years, I have found people willing to invest money in publishing a few of my books, knowing that they were taking a huge risk. Everything worth doing carries risk, and whoever helps you should do it without expecting a big payday. It's okay to hope for a big payday, but it's not okay to expect it. With those expectations, people will become disappointed and blame you for misleading them. That's a reputation you may never overcome.

Seek God to guide you to the right helpers at the right time and place. They will be blessed spiritually for helping you accomplish the thing God called you to do. The blessing is the main thing. You are laboring together for His kingdom. A financial return should be considered a bonus.

Do not be dismayed by this situation. This is actually a wonderful part of your story. Do not think small. The possibilities are endless. One way or another, you can see this happen.

BEWARE VANITY PUBLISHING

Self-publishing is one thing, vanity publishing is another. I am recommending that you self-publish and stay away from the other kind. In self-publishing you must carry your own weight, but you remain in control of your destiny. You own your copyright and are required to register it and obtain an ISBN for the title, and it is up to you to find your audience and sell books. You must make your own website. But you can start, stop, and withdraw from agreements when the circumstances call for it.

Vanity publishers have aggressive sales forces who will tell you stories of other authors making big money with them.

Most of all, they promise to take all of the worry and difficulty of publishing away from you. They will do absolutely everything for you, and you will receive your royalty check when books sell. But in the end they will own your copyright and ISBN, and you will have no option with them for the rest of your days. Forget it.

If someone tells you everything you want to hear, run the other direction. That's how to avoid major regrets.

DISTRIBUTION

Once you have a book published, it's time to make it available for sale. You can get it formatted for electronic sale through the bookmaking services. You may also have it prepared for print-on-demand and sold on Amazon.com. That means that you don't have to print a lot of books and pay for warehousing. A book is printed and shipped directly from Amazon when someone buys it, and they pay you your royalty. This is the big advantage of this digital age for self-publishers.

Also, if you have a speaking schedule to an event where you might become a celebrity for an hour, they can ship a supply of books to that venue in advance. You should always keep a supply on hand to use for publicity, to give to reviewers, and for booking media and public speaking events. The books should also be available through your website, even if they simply follow a link to Amazon for the e-book or paperback version. Whenever you have an interview, your website should be advertised as the place to find the book. Find as many places to make your book available as you possibly can. This is distribution.

But once your book is out there, you'll find your baby in the same position that I was when sitting in the back of the Anatole ballroom with Gloria Vanderbilt. People will pass by your book on their way to the next celebrity-driven bestseller. Why should they stop and pay attention to you? Is there something about you that makes your story compelling? For Nichole, it was overcoming mental and emotional disorders. For Deborah McDermott, it was defeating autism. What about you?

WHO ARE YOU?

What makes you tick? What is your passion? What would you do if money was no object? What would your family say about you? How would that differ from what your friends would say? What makes you laugh? What makes you cry? What is the defining story of your life?

When I began to craft my website at stephenbransford.com, I put myself through this discipline. Who am I? Who am I not? What has God cultivated throughout my life that can be valuable to others? What could I focus on that would never bore me? What is the main plot of my life? What are merely subplots? What is beside the point?

I knew that I couldn't be all things to all people. I had to be just one thing to the world. Something with a handle, something definable. What were the possibilities? I began taking inventory of me.

This was a months-long process drawing upon the experiences of a lifetime. At first, I couldn't see the forest for the trees.

Publishing Strategy

I had so many dreams, dramas, traumas, ecstasies, thresholds, turning points, and vehicles—the collection just seemed chaotic. But after sorting and categorizing the elements of my story, patterns began to emerge.

Finally, I found a word to define me to the world: *storyteller*. This word was not a label I pasted on myself. It had emerged organically from my entire life, having gone through many stages of development. It defined me in a way that other people could understand. I had made storytelling valuable for other people, but I saw that my ability to do that had arisen from a deep study of my own story. This is when my life's message emerged: *You've got a story, and it's better than you think.*

This is the process I recommend for you. It's more than an academic exercise; it's spiritual. It's a stewardship of the gift of life, and the gift of eternal life that you have been given. When you know who you are, you will know what to do to get people to stop at your table and buy a book. Not everyone will stop. Not all of them will appreciate who you are, but you are not to worry about that. God wants to use your story to touch the people He chooses to receive your message.

And what if many of them never care enough to stop? What if the story of your life is not exciting or compelling enough to make them look twice? What if all your effort does not result in enough book sales to pay the rent? This is when you do what Nichole did and have a deep conversation with your heavenly Father. What will He choose to do with your story? Will you let that be enough for you? Will you embrace His plan and find rest for your soul? Will you discover that the riches of heaven are not to be compared to the fleeting glory of earthly success?

GOD'S CHOICE

As I wrote this chapter during the holiday season, my 95-year-old mother suffered a stroke. My siblings were at her side. Each day they shared small Facetime visits with my wife and me via cell phone so that we could speak with her. As the days passed, I saw that she was approaching her transition to heaven. She had lived a blessed and full life in Christ. I wanted to honor her in some way.

I had visited her many times in recent years. But this year, as I visited, she had shared a very special story with me. I knew when I heard it that it was God's story of her life—a true picture of His indwelling Spirit bearing fruit in her, and I would remember it whenever I thought about my mom thereafter.

Two days after Christmas she died. Immediately I felt urged to write a testimony of her life and to tell the story that she had told me earlier. As I wrote it, I put into practice everything I have written in this book. The words began to flow, and I sensed the gifts of the Spirit at work. I posted the short, finished story on Facebook.

I have 1600 Facebook friends, 235 of them clicked and responded to the story, and 179 of them took the time to write a heartfelt message in response, several saying that the story had changed their lives. There were 3 shares. These are not numbers to impress any publisher, but they represent true ministry that God wanted to use for His eternal purpose. Her children and the hundreds who knew her nodded their heads in agreement when they read my tribute, and said, "Yes, that was Betty Bransford."

Publishing Strategy

Mom had a story, and writing this version of it pretty well summed up who she was to many of us. As I look back on it now, I feel as if it was a lifetime achievement for me as her son. Financial and publishing success does not bring fulfillment like this. Obeying the voice of the Lord does:

BETTY ELLEN (PENFIELD) BRANSFORD
Born: March 18, 1924 – With Jesus: December 27, 2019

She wanted to do more, live more, be more than her failing body would allow. She often expressed frustration at her disabilities. But when the stroke suddenly intervened a few days ago, her frustration seemed to melt away. We would talk to her and watch her struggle to reply, managing only a couple of words before lapsing into mumbles. She would hear herself speaking gibberish and laugh. What a woman! Few of us would see humor in a similar situation. Soon, however, she sank into a peaceful twilight, her responses becoming less and less, and finally imperceptible.

It was then we knew that we had enjoyed our last conversations with the woman who had loved all seven of her children with an even hand. I had always wanted to be more special to her than that, but she wouldn't think of it. Not only did she love her children equally, she loved other people's children and took them in again and again to share our family life. Over the years I have been amazed to meet strangers who still call her "Mom."

You've Got a Story

At 95 years of age, we knew Mom's heart belonged to Jesus in ways that amazed all of us. She infused our family with the ability to think the best about people. Without cynicism, she gave everyone the benefit of the doubt. Forgiving to a fault, and caring about everyone she met. Last spring she finally told me the story that explained her amazing disposition:

At nine years of age her parents moved from Vernal, UT to Hollywood so her Dad could work as a set builder at RKO Studios. A simple shoe cobbler, after a year in Hollywood he decided it wasn't for him. Upon returning to Vernal, Mom's little heart was broken as her friends all snubbed her at school. She had been to Hollywood, they had not. They literally turned their backs to her. She told her mother she would never go back to that school. But her mother gave her the advice that changed her life and guided her for the rest of her days. She said, "You go back to that school and ignore your friends. Instead, find someone that no one wants to be around, and you make them feel special. You pay attention to the one who is outcast." At lunch that day Mom found a girl eating all alone. She sat beside her and introduced herself. The girl was ashamed to show her face because she had a cleft palate. Mom made her feel special. By the end of the school year Mom was voted the most popular girl with the best personality in the entire student body. From that day until the day of her stroke, she sought the outcast, the person sitting alone at church, the person on the fringe, any stranger in the room, and she brought them

Publishing Strategy

close with a greeting that told them they were important, and they belonged.

How blessed I have been to be her second son. I'll never live long enough to absorb the full brilliance of the lesson she learned at the tender age of nine.

Stephen Bransford
December 27, 2019

Chapter Six

A FINAL WORD

I hope by now you have understood the importance of your personal story. It is the essence of the relationship that lives and breathes between you and your heavenly Father. It cannot be fully published, nor can it be fully appreciated. Not even by you. You are part mystery and part revelation. You are His parable. We are talking about the never-ending story of your life in Christ and of His life in you. Your story will only be complete in Him when you are face to face. And even then, I am convinced that an eternal destiny will blossom from the seed of the life you lay down, and your story will go on in heaven.

So, if you have really grasped this idea, then it will be easier for you to deal with the disappointments I am about to describe. I must tell you that your testimony to the world will always fall short of the beauty and wonder of your life in Christ, no matter how well you write it. Anything you publish will be subject to the erosion of the world, the flesh, and the devil. This is true if you are published by a mainstream house or if you self-publish. I have looked back at my self-published works years later and smacked myself for making mistakes that I would know how to avoid today. *Drat!* My works published by mainstream houses have likewise disappointed. It is inevitable in this world. I hope you can become comfortable with this truth. You must rest in knowing that God called you to share your story, and by His Spirit He makes it work for His purposes in ways you cannot fully see. Resting in this truth is always an act of faith.

For me this is great comfort. I think of my first screenplay, *Riders of the Long Road*, optioned for a motion picture that was ruined by the unforeseen divorce of the husband and wife producers who had purchased it.

I think then of the ordeal of turning the screenplay into an award-winning novel. It was to be the first of a planned trilogy of novels about the circuit-riding preacher in American history. When Doubleday published and I won the Texas Literary Festival, I felt sure that I had launched a career that would affect the literary culture for the kingdom of God, only to have my publisher suddenly bought by a European firm that turned its back on me and would not publish my sequel. In the meantime, I was forced to neglect writing in order to work full time to properly care for my family.

I also think of my next novel, *High Places*, a supernatural thriller written eight years later. It was chosen to follow the success of Frank Peretti's breakthrough Christian novel, *This Present Darkness*, at a Chicago publishing house. *High Places* was the first of a planned trilogy of novels springing from the biblical description of the Nephilim in Genesis. I borrowed money from my younger brother to allow me to focus on the writing. Even though it sold a career-making number of copies, my fictional treatment of the Nephilim contributed to a controversy that split the two brothers who ran the publishing house.

One brother left and joined Thomas Nelson Publishers in Nashville. He sent me a contract for the entire *High Places*

A Final Word

trilogy—my dream come true! But it sat mocking me on my desk, as his brother held the original book hostage and wouldn't release it so I could pursue my career. These were heartbreaking events beyond my control.

I think finally of that exiled brother at Thomas Nelson, who went on to publish my public testimony, *The Last Photograph*, as a consolation prize. This little hardback was my biographical treasure. As soon as the book was released, he was fired. Thomas Nelson never even put my book in their catalog. They immediately declared it "out of print" and dumped the first printing of 8000 copies into the aftermarket. The books were bought by internet scavengers, who continue to sell them on Amazon today without having to pay me a single royalty. As I said, anything you publish will be subject to the evil of the world, the flesh, and the devil.

This is true even if you meet success. Yes, even if your testimony is a bestseller and creates a career for you, it will disappoint you on some level. I have met authors who have known wild success. Their dreams came true, and they discovered them to be part nightmare. In one case, a Christian novelist, who became a bestseller and was courted by Hollywood, has now fallen into a life-ending alcoholic haze. Others who have learned to ride the wave of success have found it a prison that dictates they continue to write only the genre that launched their original bestseller. Depart from it, and publishers will ignore you as if you are a novice. There are some happy exceptions to this rule, but they are as rare as rocking horse poo.

Why is success so disappointing? Because everyone who is lifted on the viral tsunami of success knows something in the depths of their soul—*they didn't make it happen.* It was an accident.

It was a coincidence of timing, of cultural appetite for their topic, of a publisher's gamble, and some kind of celebrity endorsement. And suddenly it's on their shoulders to make it all happen again. This can drive some to drink. Or to other forms of comfort.

Take James Michener for example: As the review copies of my historical novel, *Riders of the Long Road*, came out, friends of mine arranged for me to pick up the famous author at the Hilton Hotel in Dallas. I was to accompany him to a Republican Party event sponsored by the Christian Coalition. He was arrogant, abrupt, and rude to me through the entire meeting. He seemed to despise the Christian political right, and it showed in his attitude and his comments.

I knew that his novels, like *Hawaii*, were famous for magnifying the worst elements of Christian history as if they were the *only* elements. He seemed of the same mind as Sinclair Lewis, who had written *Elmer Gantry*, the novel that had inspired me to write fiction at age sixteen.

Back at the Hilton, just before exiting my car, he turned to me and said, "My wife read your novel. She said it was good."

My publisher had been hoping Michener would endorse me. Instead, I felt like he had just thrown me a bone. "Thank you," I said. "I used Francis Asbury's journals as my principal source." I wanted him to know that I had been diligent to represent history according to the journals of the original American circuit-riding preacher.

He nodded. "I used those journals when I wrote *Chesapeake*. But you may be the only author I know who finds the circuit-riding preacher to be a sympathetic character."

A Final Word

I'm pretty sure he meant it as an insult. I took it as a compliment. I had at least made some small mark against the prejudice of the literary establishment.

He then slapped me with his *coup de grace*: "So, you've written one novel, young man. I've written thirty-three bestsellers. Do you think you can write another? That's what separates the men from the boys."

As he walked away, I was reminded that what also separated men from boys, at least in his case, was a team of paid researchers who were helping him compile his epic novel *Texas* at the time. Why would a super-successful author like him feel the need to put down a beginner like me?

Success does not bring contentment. Something else does. I say it is knowing your story in Christ. That is the true epic that will never disappoint. With this kind of perspective, you can let go of your published works and release them to God. Success or failure is ultimately in His hands. Man does his best, but God is the Lord of the harvest. If you don't believe this, you have set yourself up for disappointment and insecurity.

I can tell you that in every case of my original published works—*Riders of the Long Road*, *High Places*, and *The Last Photograph*—God has let me know that He has worked it all for my good and for His purposes, in spite of the publishing setbacks. Many lives have been deeply touched and affected. Some of the people whose lives have been touched have communicated with me. Most of them I will never know in this life. And that's okay because my story, my relationship with God, has come to mean so much more to me than my published works. That is the primary lesson I want to share with you in this book. This is true success, and as you seek to write your story, I urge you to seek first His kingdom.

You've got a story, and it *is* better than you think.

ABOUT THE AUTHOR

Stephen Bransford is Director of Media Production for Andrew Wommack Ministries and Charis Bible College. He attended Bethany Bible College before earning an English degree from Arizona State University. He has provided various communication services for Billy Graham, Bill Bright, Oral Roberts, Reinhard Bonnke, James Robison, the Assemblies of God, the United Methodist Church, the Boy Scouts of America, and many others. He is an award-winning Christian author, with novels published by Doubleday, Crossway, and Thomas Nelson, and a ghostwriter with books translated and distributed worldwide. In 1999, he launched Andrew Wommack on television through the *Gospel Truth* broadcast, reaching just 3% of the U.S. audience. Today, the program reaches a potential audience of 3.4 billion worldwide. He writes a blog on storytelling, self-discovery, and transformation at **www.stephenbransford.com**.

Novels by Stephen Bransford

Riders of the Long Road
The Last Photograph
High Places

Printed by Amazon Italia Logistica S.r.l.
Torrazza Piemonte (TO), Italy